Penguin Books
Home Before Night

Hugh Leonard was born in Dublin in 1926 and was educated
at Presentation College, Dun Laoghaire, and then spent
fourteen years as a clerk in the Land Commission. He was
able to give up this job when he began to have some success
as a playwright. He was Literary Editor of the Abbey Theatre
from 1976 until 1977, and has been Programme Director of
the Dublin Theatre Festival since 1978. His earlier plays
include *A Leap in the Dark* (1957), *A Walk on the Water* (1960),
The Saints Go Cycling In (1965), *The Au Pair Man* (1968), *The
Patrick Pearse Motel* (1971), *Thieves* (1973), *Summer* (1974),
Irishmen (1975), and *Time Was* (1976). His real breakthrough
came with *Da*, which in the United States won a Tony
Award for the Best Play of 1978, the Drama Desk Award and
the New York Critics' Circle Award. He also won the Harvey
Award for the best play of 1979–80 with *A Life*. (Penguin
have published *Da*, *A Life* and *Time Was* in one volume.)
Among his more recent plays are *Moving Days*, *Kill*,
Scorpions (three stage plays) and *The Mask of Moriarty*. He
has also written plays for television, including *Silent Song*,
which won the Italia Award for 1967, *The Last Campaign*, *The
Ring and the Rose* and *A Life*. His adaptations for television
include *Nicholas Nickleby*, *Wuthering Heights*, *Strumpet City*,
The Little World of Don Camillo, *O'Neill*, *The Irish RM* and
Troubles. He lives in Dublin.

Hugh Leonard

Home Before Night

Penguin Books

PENGUIN BOOKS

Published by the Penguin Group
27 Wrights Lane, London W8 5TZ, England
Viking Penguin Inc., 40 West 23rd Street, New York, New York 10010, USA
Penguin Books Australia Ltd, Ringwood, Victoria, Australia
Penguin Books Canada Ltd, 2801 John Street, Markham, Ontario, Canada L3R 1B4
Penguin Books (NZ) Ltd, 182–190 Wairau Road, Auckland 10, New Zealand

Penguin Books Ltd, Registered Offices: Harmondsworth, Middlesex, England

First published by André Deutch Ltd 1979
Published in Penguin Books 1981
10 9 8 7 6 5

Phototypeset in Great Britain by
Filmtype Services Ltd, Scarborough
Printed and bound in Great Britain by
Cox & Wyman Ltd, Reading
Set in Monophoto Photina

To my parents

Chapter 1

My grandmother made dying her life's work. I remember her as a vast malevolent old woman, so obese that she was unable to wander beyond the paved yard outside her front door. Her pink-washed cottage had two rooms and she agonized her way through and around them, clutching at the furniture for support and emitting heart-scalding gasps, as if death was no further off than the dresser or the settle bed where my uncle Sonny slept himself sober. In those days people confused old age with valour; they called her a great old warrior. This had the effect of inspiring her to gasp even more distressingly by way of proving them right and herself indomitable. In case her respiratory noises should come to be as taken for granted as the ticking of the clock (which at least stopped now and then), she provided a contrapuntal accompaniment by kicking the chairs, using the milk jugs as cymbals and percussing the kettle and frying pan.

To be fair, it was her only diversion. The rent-man, peering in over the half-door, would suffer like a damned soul as she counted out three shillings and ninepence in coppers, threepenny bits and sixpences, wheezing a goodbye to each coin, and then began her tortured *via dolorosa* towards him, determined to pay her debts before dropping dead at his feet, a martyr to landlordism. Even Dr Enright was intimidated. When he had listened to her heartbeats it was not his stethoscope but her doomed slaughterhouse eyes imploring the worst which caused him to tell her: 'Sure we've all got to go some day, ma'am.' That pleased her. Privately, she saw no reason why she should go at any time, but she liked to nod submissively, essay a practice death-rattle and resignedly endorse the will of the Almighty.

She dressed in shiny black and wore a brooch inscribed 'Mother'. Her girth almost exceeded her stature, and her prodigious appetite amazed me, for her cooking verged on the poisonous: in fact, I have known no other woman who could make fried eggs taste like perished rubber. On the occasions when my mother deposited me at Rosanna Cottage for the day, the midday meal consisted unvaryingly of fried egg and potatoes. I was too afraid of her baleful eyes to refuse to eat, so would get rid of the accursed egg by balancing it on the blade of my knife and swallowing it whole. This she came to interpret as a tribute to her culinary powers and, as my eyes streamed and gorge rose, would set about frying me another egg.

Her husband, a casual labourer, had died suddenly in 1926 after cleaning out a cesspit. They had four children: Sonny, Mary, Christine and Margaret, my mother. Sonny, who lived at home, courted a laundress named Kate Fortune for more than thirty years and finally married her when the will of God at last prevailed over that of my grandmother. By then the lovers were in their mid-fifties. Kate Fortune was sheep-faced, bony and as tall – above six feet – as Sonny was short. She exuded a perpetual dampness, which I always ascribed to her labours in the Dargle Laundry, and was permitted to cross my grandmother's threshold only at Christmas. She would sit, dumbly miserable, the heiress presumptive to the cottage and on that account hated, trying to find a hiding place for the marzipan from the home-baked Christmas cake. Even Sonny came to ignore her, for she grew plainer and bonier by the year. Once, such was her hurry to be off and catch the Bray bus home that she forgot to stoop and banged her head against the lintel. She cried out and slid to the ground, folding at the joints this way and that like an anchor chain and clutching her forehead. When Sonny pulled her hand away to examine the injury, a viscous grey slime oozed down between her eyes, and at first we thought that she had dashed her brains out. Then we realized it was squashed marzipan which she had been concealing in her fist.

Less from choice than necessity, Kate went on toiling in the laundry after she and Sonny were married. His life had always been encompassed by the labour exchange, Dowling's betting office and Larkin's public house, and it seemed only commonsense to him that for Kate to cease work and for him to commence would be a case of robbing Peter to pay Paul. Also, as he pointed out, to disrupt the balance of nature so late in life, could be injurious to their systems. He had dark, disappointed eyes. He stood in Gilbey's doorway which commanded a view of Castle Street and nodded curtly at passers-by, knowing that every one of them would do him down if given the chance. His shortness was aggravated by a hoppity limp which obliged him to stand at attention with one leg and at ease with the other, and was caused, so my father told me – perhaps apocryphally – by Sonny having fallen asleep in the lavatory for six hours when the worse for drink. There was a long narrow lane leading to Rosanna Cottage, and there I found him once, standing erect but unconscious, his head embedded in the depths of a prickly hedge. The smell of stale porter constantly enveloped him like a caul, and, in common with the other Doyles, in drink or out of it he was a ready enemy. Forget to salute him in the town, and your name was scrawled indelibly in the black book of his brain. When he limped out of the betting office and tore up his docket, there was a smell of anger as well as of porter. He would smile, biding his hour against the hidden beings who had denied him a fair crack of life's whip.

His sister Mary lived at home, too. While Sonny slept like a coffined corpse in the settle bed, dreaming of old hurts and new enemies, she shared the other room with my grandmother and snored in the red glow of the Sacred Heart lamp. She had the mental age of a seven-year-old and was the prey of gangs of boys who chanted 'Mad Mary!' in her wake. Her vocabulary on those occasions would strip paint from a hall door. Curses, oaths and imprecations would hailstorm on her persecutors, but at home she was angelic. My grandmother doted upon her and was given to saying that while the rest of us would be lucky to escape hell by the short hairs, Mary's place with the saints was assured. Personally, I had doubts: particularly when Mary would slam a door on my fingers or deliver a rabbit-punch to the kidneys when unobserved. My aggrieved howls were wasted. Mary screwed her eyes up so that only the whites showed and gave such an astonishingly adept portrayal of slandered sanctity that I earned one clout across the face for lying and a second for tormenting the afflicted.

Often, she was entrusted with a simple errand as far as Mrs Toole's shop on the Barrack Road, and extravagant hosannas were sung when she arrived home skipping like a carefree young hippo and swinging a shopping bag which had probably disfigured any name-callers imprudent enough to venture within range. 'Amn't I good?' she would inquire archly, the pupils of her eyes disappearing towards the rear of her skull, and my grandmother would weep agreement. There was weeping of another kind, however, the day Mary disappeared.

I can remember only the lamentation, not the circumstances. The house was blue with policemen, for once friendly. My mother wept; my grandmother lay on her bed like a capsized Alp, her death-grunts escalating in tempo and volume until they fused and became a steady rumble that shook the house; while Sonny, in his element, swore that he would swing for the man who had tampered with his sister. 'Tamper with *that?*' my father muttered under his breath. For myself, I was not sure what tampering involved, unless Mary, like the mechanical man in *The Invisible Ray*, which was the follower-upper at the Picture House in Dun Laoghaire, was unsuspectedly equipped with controls which someone had interfered with.

While the neighbours hunted through the town, Sonny stood outside the lavatory in the yard crashing his fists, handcuffed together by grief, against the door and moaning, 'My lovely sister.' That evening, as hope waned, he evolved a theory and found a suspect. There was, in the town, a respectable frizzy-haired man named Finnerty who ran the diddlum society. Every Friday evening my father went to his house to plank down a shilling against the Christmas Eve payout of two pounds ten. People would linger just to watch Mr Finnerty, like a rajah, his back to the roaring fire, piling up silver towers of money on the velveteen tablecloth and making slanting pen strokes in his ledger. Many years previously, the town had been appalled and entertained by the depredations of a mysterious being who lurked in unlit laneways and leaped out at passing females. No drastic harm was done, except perhaps to the nervous system of one middle-aged Child of Mary, and the attacker became known locally as the Long Fella from the description of another of his victims, who had seen his shadow stretch the width of the Convent Road an instant before his hand darted under her skirt and broke her knicker-elastic. In time, the attacks ceased. It was rumoured that the police had at last caught him at it and warned him to be a good man and stop the codology. It was further rumoured that the Long Fella was none other than Mr Finnerty, who was only five-foot-five, if that, and now had a windmill in his back garden and ran the diddlum.

That was years in the past, but the idea got caught like a fishhook in my uncle Sonny's brain that the Long Fella had come out of retirement and struck again. There was a dark side, I think, to Sonny's nature. When he looked at others he saw his own blackness in them, like a man wearing smoked glasses who remarks on how dismal the day is. Mary's body, he knew beyond contradiction, was under the gorse on Dalkey Hill or in Dekko's Cave or bobbing in the sea off the Lady's Well. It was useless for my father – who in any case became incoherent when he tried to be reasonable – to point out that breaking a woman's elastic was a long day's journey from (with a look at me) getting down to business. 'Aye,' Sonny said with a crooked smile, 'but how do hens know the size of eggcups?' And, leaving us to ponder on that conundrum, he went hopping down the path and to Larkin's, where he drank four pints of plain in between inciting the regulars to march with him on Mr Finnerty's house.

Not one of them believed that Mary, who was a great shapeless lump of a woman, had been overpowered by little Mr Finnerty. Against that, it was rarely they got the chance of demonstrating their abhorrence of crimes of lust; so after leisurely discussion and a show of hands it was agreed that if Sonny would only contain himself until closing time, those present would accompany him in the roles of disinterested observers. As Gunger Hammond remarked: 'If he's done it to her, where's the differ in another hour?'

A small crowd duly set out for Mr Finnerty's small neat house on the Bus Lawn, with Sonny four hops ahead of them. I was eight at the time, and he reminded me of the burgomaster leading the mob in *The Bride of Frankenstein*. But his interlude in Larkin's had cost him the advantage of surprise: the door was locked and bolted, not a light showed. The crowd took up a detached attitude from Sonny at a distance which would absolve them of complicity, and watched him open the proceedings by shouting 'Come out, you whoor-master' through the letterbox and banging on the front door with his short leg. When he showed signs of flagging, the odd word of encouragement from the rear refuelled his fury.

'One of yous gimme a brick,' he demanded, and seemed taken aback to be handed one immediately. He took aim at the front window, but instead of letting fly, embarked on a series of practice throws, rushing towards the house with an elliptical up and down gait like the oscillating-arm on a piston and stabbing the air with the brick. After several minutes of this, the crowd grew restive and a voice reminded Sonny that some of them had homes to go to. 'Who said that?' Sonny roared, seizing on the diversion.

Oats Nolan stepped forward and addressed him coolly. '*I* didn't. But if you're going to break the man's window, then for the love of God break the man's window and stop jack-acting.' Another voice said that if there was one thing he couldn't abide it was a mouth.

Sonny, in a cleft stick, had the choice of either losing face and perhaps one of the few teeth left in his head by turning his wrath on the malcontents, or of committing the enormity of breaking the window of a man who, when all was said and done, was the prefect of Sonny's guild in the Men's Sodality. As he wavered, two things happened. His audience began to disperse in disgust, and a policeman emerged leisurely from the shadow of Findlater's clock at the corner. It was a question of honour. With a cry of 'Whoormaster!' Sonny vanished down the laneway which led to the rear of the house. The crowd, its expectations restored, surged after him and were in time to see him take hold of Mr Finnerty's windmill and shake it savagely. It was a high girdered structure, designed to provide an auxiliary supply of electricity, and no one was more surprised than Sonny to see it fall sideways and, to the accompaniment of screams from the house, crash through the roof of the back scullery. As the policeman shouldered his way through the awed crowd, Sonny nodded bitterly at the mangled windmill, as if it, like everyone else, existed only to do him down.

As for Mary, she arrived home by the last tram. It transpired that she, whose expeditions to Toole's shop two hundred yards away were acclaimed as small miracles of survival, had abstracted two pounds from my grandmother's mattress and caught a tram to Booterstown. There, on a piece of waste ground, Toft's yearly fun fair splintered the night with noise, and she had spent every penny – except, cunningly, her fare home – on sixpenny rides on the roundabout and chairoplanes. Deliriously shouting 'Woosh, Maria!' to the crowds below, she had clung to the painted mane of a rearing horse or soared through the dark at the end of groaning chains. A neighbour's first sight of her was as she thudded homewards along Sorrento Road, beret askew and one black woollen stocking around her ankle.

There was desolation, of course: not least on account of the incarcerated Sonny. The proof that Mary was not as mad as we had imagined gave my grandmother no comfort. She raged, choked, called her a thief and a rip, and threatened her with Father Creedon, who would ask God as a special favour to make an exception in Mary's case and consign her to hell's hottest hob. Mary bore the chastisement with serenity. Then, as if damnation in the next world were not enough, my grandmother cancelled a promised outing for the following Sunday: tea at my aunt Chris's house.

At this, Mary left off inspecting the inside of her cranium and shoved a bunched fist under my grandmother's nose. 'I *am* goin'.'

'You're not, you faggot you.'

'I am, I am.'

'I say you're not.'

'I will.'

'You won't.'

Mary looked at her in baffled rage, then said triumphantly: 'Well, I won't go at all, so!' and locked herself in the outside lav.

The police, not wanting Sonny for an enemy, released him the following morning. It was agreed that he pay a half-crown each week out of his dole money towards the restoration of the windmill and the scullery: which he did until Mr Finnerty tired of chasing him for it. What annoyed Sonny most about the affair was not being dunned for payment, but that Mr Finnerty had made a fool of him by not tampering with Mary.

My aunt Chris was the success of the family. She made the most of her dark plumpness and cured herself of the adenoidal Dalkey accent which made two syllables out of one. Either by instinct or design, she cultivated a demureness which was tinged with a hint of banked inner fires. She was ambitious. She may have lived in a labourer's cottage, but she heard the Dublin trains beyond the back wall and saw the engine smoke swirl and curtsey over Sonny's weedy ridges of potatoes and swedes; and she knew what she wanted. No hobnailed lad from the town ever got his arm around her shirtwaist or drew the long pins from her flat straw boater or walked her along the Metals with its sin-blest patches of indented grass. She was a bird-alone. Women in doorways eyed her sourly and said that she had gotten above herself. She made no answer: unlike the other Doyles, she knew how to hold her tongue. She had no strong likes or dislikes: for her, people and things were not so much bad or good as vulgar or tasteful.

Her quietness and good manners were mistaken by members of the local quality for indications that she knew her place. One of them – a Miss Tyson – recommended Chris to a Dublin milliner, and so it happened that as a reward for knowing her station in life she was enabled to rise above it. The irony was lost on Chris: she had watched and waited, and she had won. The most her friends in The Dwellings or the Alley Lane could expect was to become kitchen maids or dailies and to marry from one slum into another. Not she, not now. She walked out on Sundays with her new friends from the milliner's: not in Dalkey where she was known, but on the East Pier at Dun Laoghaire, where the brass band drew ripples of genteel applause and ladies sacrificed the view from the upper promenade for the modesty of the lower. The moan of the mailboat siren vied with the sounds of gulls, waves and Suppé. It was on one such Sunday that she met John Bennett.

When he tipped his hat, Chris saw a round bald head and, under it, the pink cheeks of a cherub. He wore gold-rimmed glasses and was a civil servant in the Land Commission: a lowly one, but nonetheless a person who began work at ten and ended it at four-thirty and wore a dark suit and collar and tie on weekdays. His fingernails shone. He invited Chris and her friend to take tea with him at the Pavilion, a dazzling white pleasure-house, ringed by balconies and sprouting with turrets: more like a ship than a building. He addressed her as 'Miss Doyle' and held the chair as she sat. Her face burned: it occurred to her that one of the waitresses might hail her familiarly as an old friend. The moment passed. She noticed that John's hands were as pink as his face. When she volunteered the remark that the colours of the bunting overhead were tasteful, he beamed and said: 'Just so.' It was his favourite expression. As they parted, he asked Chris if she would care to accompany him to the Horse Show the following Saturday. Watching him set off along the sea front, she felt as if she were a passenger on a tram and the conductor had called out her destination. She was captivated, not least by his meekness and gentle voice, and it was some time before she discovered that he bore and had richly earned the nickname of 'Curser' Bennett.

In the Land Commission, John's addiction to rainbow-hued profanity was legendary, especially since his obscenities were uttered like benisons. Lady typists were a recent innovation, but none was permitted to set foot on his landing – not since the day he unthinkingly dropped a noggin bottle of whiskey into a desk drawer which lacked a bottom. The bottle broke, and in a panic-stricken attempt to get rid of the smell before his superior walked in, he emptied the contents of a fire bucket on the floor, which at once became awash with dirty water reeking of seven-year-old malt. His observations on that occasion, proceeding as they did from the lips of a Botticelli baby angel, caused a typist to run shrieking into Merrion Street.

To Chris, however, he was dapper, gentle and devoted. His ardour even survived the necessary evil of meeting his future in-laws.

My grandmother's reaction to his impending visit was to declare stonily that he could like the Doyles or lump them. They were the old Dalkey stock, tried and true, nobody's coachmen, owing nothing to no one. 'We won't,' she said, 'pretend to be what we're not.' She then proceeded to scrub the dresser, blacklead the range, wash the window curtains and change the stagnant holy water in the font by the door. Sonny, characteristically, did some detective work. Apart from the possibility that John might turn out to be a sex maniac, Sonny's unvarying attitude towards persons unknown was to discover their weaknesses, thereby establishing his own moral, social or physical superiority. He was unlucky. The only known crime in John's family dossier was the defection of a distant cousin to the Church of Ireland. This put Sonny in a foul humour all week, but he cheered up on the Sunday when the paragon arrived and proved to be prematurely bald.

Once the introductions were made, John was deposited on the chair nearest the fire. His eyes smarted from the turf smoke, but Chris saw no indication of the dismay she had dreaded. He gave her a red-rimmed blink of reassurance and nodded amiably at Sonny, who was staring at John's shining head with a scornful half-smile of inner mirth. My grandfather, near asphyxia from an unaccustomed starched collar, launched into the kind of small talk he considered appropriate to mixed company: specifically, the more lubricious details of the Kaiser's alleged atrocities in Belgium. John nodded affably and said: 'Just so.'

Then Sonny, unable to restrain himself any longer, remarked jocularly: 'That's a fine head of skin you have there.'

The moon that was John's face glowed upon him. A particle of turf dust was flicked from a grey spat. 'Baldness doesn't run in our family, you know,' John said apologetically. 'My hair simply fell out.' He sighed, then added, just as amicably: 'Like your teeth.' He turned back to my grandfather and said: 'The Kaiser. Oh, an uncivilized man. Just so.'

The afternoon was further punctuated by Mary's determination to make a lasting impression on Chris's intended. She produced her toy perambulator and her dolls, serenading them with 'Daisy, Daisy': the only song she knew, until she somehow memorized the words of 'Over the Rainbow' more than twenty years later. Becoming bolder, she gave John great bruising nudges of complicity, accompanied by blood-curdling leers, and even clamped a hand like a saucepan lid upon his pate in approbation. Sonny, who had taken the reference to his dental deficiencies with ill grace, sulked throughout the afternoon, having confided to Chris that John was a damn sight too pass-remarkable for his liking.

The first sight of John, embellished by spats, cane, tie-pin and gold Albert, had reduced my grandmother to awe. She would have gladly believed it had Chris introduced him as the late King Edward, incognito and cleanshaven; and it was only at teatime when the conversation turned to the subject of his weak stomach that she regained a measure of her assertiveness. While Chris served him with two three-minute eggs (knowing where danger lay, she had insisted on preparing them herself), John explained that his digestive system could tolerate no foods stronger than boiled fish and milk puddings. My grandmother had a mental picture of herself as possessing a mixture of gruffness and lovable commonsense. 'Wisha, go 'long out of that!' she cried, and informed him that indigestion was all in the mind and that if shoe leather was properly cooked it would not take a feather out of him. As Chris turned white, she cleared his boiled eggs from the table and duly presented him with a toxic high tea of rashers, sausages and the remnants of the cabbage from dinner time, all under a widow's veil of opaque grease. By the time he unburdened himself of the meal from the open top deck of a number 8 tram later that evening, the match between Chris and himself had been made, and my grandmother had bestowed upon him her supreme accolade: the title of 'a great favourite'.

They married. I am not sure of how or when Chris became aware of his gift for execration, but at work his language gradually shed its lustre. Within a few years he was almost wholly Dr Jekyll, and it was in 1922 that Mr Hyde made his farewell appearance. The Civil War had ended and all civil servants were compelled, under pain of dismissal, to take a formal oath of allegiance to the new Free State government. Most of them, including John, did so, but a few refused out of rebel sympathies. One of these diehards was a man appropriately named Thunder, and on the day of his departure an office party was given in his honour by those of his colleagues who, while applauding his principles, believed that as far as they themselves were concerned patriotism could be carried to excess. Wives were invited, and the revelry spread through several offices.

John was in vintage form. In Chris's absence, he cursed the government, be-Jasused the Free State, effed the oath of allegiance, blinded the Irish language and cast serious doubts on the paternity of the Minister for Lands. His pink cheeks became infused with an angry sunset glow as he downed proffered tumblers of John Jameson, and a shout went up that he should grace the occasion with the recitation for which, in his bachelor days, he had become famous whenever gripped by strong emotion. Eager hands hoisted him to a table top, and for the last time in his life, with glass thrust high, he began to declaim the poem, 'Fontenoy':

> 'Thrice at the huts of Fontenoy the British column failed,
> And twice the lines of St Antoine the Dutch in vain
> assailed ...'

He never reached the line which unfailingly brought the house down –

> 'Not yet, my liege,' Saxe interposed, 'the Irish troops
> remain!' –

for the door opened and my aunt Chris stepped in and said quietly: 'No politics, John. Home now.'

Then Curser Bennett climbed down from the table and nodded amicably to his colleagues. John Bennett followed Chris from the room.

The phrase, 'No politics, John', was to become an incantation through the years. It nipped countless arguments, on the point of becoming convivially strenuous, in the bud, and I have known it to fail only once: at Sonny's wedding, when John had already been dragged out of earshot. He was taken from the house 'on a message' by the low element which afflicts every wedding day, and was borne back five hours later, face downwards and singing 'Little Dolly Daydream' to the pavement.

In fairness to Chris, she was a tireless wife. His suits were immaculate, his linen was changed daily, his shoes resembled mirrors. He wore a scarf from October to May. His colds were soothed with vapour rubs and syrups; his diet was supervised. The heady aroma of floor wax filled their house like incense. Ornaments were positioned with deadly symmetry lest the slightest imbalance should cause the walls to collapse. Inside the front door, carpet slippers were in readiness for John's return from work, the heels facing him.

They kept to themselves, except for duty visits to our house and to my grandmother's. Every summer they spent two weeks at Greystones, a sedate resort ten miles away, and walked the length of the sea front to the harbour and back again, rarely speaking, or sat in the hotel conservatory reading their *Irish Independent*. (Once, at home, a copy of the *Irish Press* arrived by mistake, and my aunt bade me return it to the newsagent with the message, never delivered, that she did not take 'rags'.)

As they grew into old age they acquired the nickname locally of the Duke and Duchess of Windsor. John's youthful follies had lost him promotion, and he left the Land Commission as he had entered it, with the grade of paper-keeper; but he and Chris comported themselves like exiled royalty. I saw them the other day, now in their eighties, walking slowly together on the sea front at Dun Laoghaire. (It was somehow in character that they should live in one Victorian seaside town and spend their holidays in another.) John was swaddled in overcoat, woollen muffler, tweed cap and over-shoes: plumper and pinker than ever; Chris wore a high-buttoned grey coat with a fur collar. They walked arm in arm. She said something and he replied: probably with a 'Just so'. I avoided them, partly because, looking into Chris's face I see my mother's again.

They are childless. For that matter, none of the Doyles of Chris's generation had children – including my mother.

Chapter 2

'If you're bold,' his mother said to him, 'I'll give you back to your mother.'

They were on the *Royal Iris*, on one of the evening cruises around Howth, and he was looking at Lambay Island. 'There she is,' his mother said, 'coming for to get you,' and real as real he saw a tall woman in black clothes on the edge of the cliffs. Her face was dark because she knew he was safe from her on the *Royal Iris*, but she would get him yet.

Later on when he grew up and got sense he would suppose that it was one of the times his mother, not his real one, but the one he called mammy, had drink on her, or why else would she frighten him? Sure enough, a man asked her up to dance with him to the melodeon band, and she went – that was proof – and he and his da sat on one of the life rafts and watched. His da said nothing then, but he must have been jealous. He had a temper; he was short with red hair and in his time had played tug-o'-war. And he had gone into a rage that day when Jack stuck his head into a Jewman's car on the Barrack Road to find out what the driver could see in the mirror.

The Jewman was off up the Alley Lane collecting payments, but his dog was in the car and it sprang up and swung out at Jack's lip. One woman ran out of her house with iodine and another with Lourdes water, and when his da came home from work Jack was wearing a moustache of sticking plaster and cotton wool and belching from the whole bottle of Taylor-Keith lemonade the Jewman had poured into him outside the hospital. 'Now, Nick,' was all his mother had time to say before his da began jumping up and down, munching his tongue and giving an imitation of a boy skipping like a lunatic along the footpath, which was how he thought Jack had cut his lip. 'He won't be marked,' his mother said as the clay from his da's boots hit the Blessed Virgin like sleet. 'Acting the go-boy, acting the go-boy,' his da sang, doing a war dance. 'You old madman,' his mother said, 'a dog bit him.' 'A nawg mih me,' Jack said, with his top lip starched into a sneer, and even when his da at last understood he was too headstrong to own himself in the wrong, but instead went jazz-dancing out into the yard and up a heap of coal. When he came back in he was in a good humour but pale from the shock. He looked at Jack on the edge of the big double bed, and said: 'Do you know what I'm going to tell you? The Kerry Blue and the alsatian is treacherous animals.'

On the *Royal Iris*, however, he watched Jack's mother waltzing with the man to 'Gold and Silver' and held his tongue. The times she had a drop taken, she was like uncle Sonny: she would go for you if you vexed her, so maybe it was as well to be jealous in your mind and not to her face. Except at Myra Kinsella's wedding, Jack had never seen her dance before. She was small and stout, like two Christmas puddings, one sitting on top of the other, with a weenchy little one on top of them again. Her hair was long and black and done up in a bun under her hat with the wide mauve band and the not-real rose. She was light on her feet. The sea was choppy, and empty stout bottles skithered up and down the wet deck, with the dancers kicking at them accidentally on purpose. A man and a girl fell, and a woman called out 'He can't wait,' whatever that meant. Jack wondered if the man would bring his mother back to them, then he looked out across the sea to Lambay Island, and away again quickly before he could see his real mother where the cliffs began. His da's red whiskers shivered in the wind.

When the dancing stopped, a man got up to sing 'Smilin' Through' and Jack's mother came back. She wasn't too bad: you could only tell if you knew her, because the eyes were queer. She would put you in mind of that woman in the pictures who always acted the mother and had the same look in her eyes, only nobody in the picture with her ever let on they noticed. When Jack saw that look – on a Holy Thursday when she came in from doing the Seven Churches, or in Christmas week, or on a bank holiday like now – he would go sulky and be cool with her. That was always the start, and she knew the signs in him as well as he knew them in her. Now, coming through the crowd on the deck, she caught sight of his face and his da's. She began to hum to show them she had not a care in the world and they were only begrudgers. Instead of sitting with them on the life raft, she plucked her handbag from between them and went off to the lav. Jack knew there was a Baby Power in the handbag, but it would be another four or five years before he would get up the nerve to open her bag at such times and pour the whiskey down the shore in the yard.

'There's Ireland's Eye, son,' his da said.

The ship was turning to go around the tip of Howth and home into Dublin Bay, and the black smoke from the funnel blew all over the deck like when you stood on the railway bridge at Dalkey. The ship's engines pounded and the crowd was joining in with 'Smilin' Through', as if it was some old come-all-ye. Jack had seen the picture. It had your woman in it, Norma Shearer. She got shot. He knew all the film stars because his mother was great for pictures: she took him to the Picture House every Monday and Friday, and his da went with them on Sundays when the serial was on. Her favourite was Marie Dressler, but she would enjoy any old film except the ones where the men had top hats on and got divorces. Jack dreaded Marie Dressler: she always made you go red by carrying on abominable in front of high-up people. She would give a nice and polite woman at a party a puck on the bare back and say that she reminded her of gin-swigging tobaccer-chewing side-winding old Chinatown Lil back in Frisco who could hit a spittoon all the way to Sacramento and never miss. This would make her son ashamed of her after she had slaved to rear him and Jack's mother would cry buckets and say to the old ones around her in the picture house: 'The more you do for them the more they turn on you.' The old ones would say that she had never said a truer word and give slanty looks at Jack as if he was the son up on the screen. He would sink low in the seat and put the blame on Marie Dressler, who was an old faggot. He hated Fredric March, too, because he always got killed in the end, and Sylvia Sidney on account of she was always crying her eyes out. She had the face for it, with everything sideways like a Chinawoman, and when she started her whingeing the cornerboys in the hard seats beyond the partition would imitate her, and Drummond the usher would shine his torch on them, but he would only put you out for calling him 'Bulldog'. Jack's favourite was Fay Wray: he had seen her all in colour in *The Mystery of the Wax Museum* with your man, Lionel Atwill, which had frightened the life out of him. When Fay Wray was in a film, it meant she would get the clothes torn off of her: it would give you a start, like someone

21

striking a match inside of you. His mother would not mind, because it was not like exposing yourself on purpose: she would say: 'The poor creature, look at the cut of her.' It was no matter to her that Fay Wray was going to have wax poured over her or was being chased by the gets with the big dogs in *The Hounds of Zaroff*: it was the good clothes in flitters that preyed on her mind. She was a funny woman. When they went to see Walter Abel in *The Three Musketeers*, with your men wearing britches and fighting with swords, she said: 'They done this film a long time ago.' You would get sick telling her.

When she came back from the lav they were passing the Bailey lighthouse. Lambay Island had gone behind Howth, and he could look out at the sea now with his two eyes, instead of keeping the near one shut like when he would run past the red Sacred Heart lamp in the window of the room where Biddy Byrne had died. 'We thought you got stuck,' his da said to his mother, to make a joke. 'No fear of me,' she said, as cold as rain. She was black out with the pair of them, and gave Jack a quick look with her bright, not-well eyes to let him know that he was a cur and she was done with him. 'The day held out fine, after all,' his da said, to be sociable. 'If a body was let enjoy it,' she said. The words fell out of her mouth the way you would chop logs with a hatchet. His da said she was a comical woman and stood Jack up on the life raft to see Dublin.

The sun was in their eyes and Dublin was as jet black as the mountains, but you could see Dun Laoghaire harbour and make out Dalkey by the island and the three hills. Home was a long way.

His mother nearly turned her ankle getting off the *Royal Iris* at Butt Bridge. Jack was with his da at the bottom of the gangway. 'Come on, Mag,' his da said. Instead, she gave a scalding look to a man who was behind her with a bottle of stout in his fist, and said: 'Don't you push me, you pup.'

The man could not believe she meant him. 'I never laid hand nor glove on you missus,' he said. The pair of them were blocking the gangway, with the crowds of the world trying to get past. The people who were already off the boat and on the quay turned to gawk. 'You're a liar and a blasted one,' his mother said.

The man had black hairs all over his face and a nose that would cut butter. He was up from the country, and all he could think of to say was: 'Who's a liar?' A high-up sailor in a peaked cap said for the passengers to move along now, please. The crowd behind his mother and the man were muttering and shoving. His da called out 'Mag, Mag,' and Jack felt his insides go empty with shame. This put Marie Dressler in the ha'penny place; it was worse, even, than the day his mother tripped and fell outside Thomas's dairy and her hat rolled along like a hoop.

'Keep your mawsy hands to yourself,' she said to the man. 'How dare you, how dare the ignorant likes of you interfere with me?'

People from off the bogs were always dangerous and would turn on you when riz, and now that the man had got a hold on his senses he went red under the black hairs. 'Don't you call me ignorant, missus,' he said in the sort of sing-song way they talked in the country. 'And I'm no liar neither, so I'm not.'

'Ignorant liar,' she said up into his face, putting the two words together to aggravate him two times over.

The edge of his nose could have stabbed her. A man who was with him caught his shoulder and said: 'Don't put yourself in a passion, Dominic. The woman has drink took.'

'I what? I what?' she said, turning on the other man 'Say that out loud.' The words were not out of her mouth when the crowd trying to get off the ship gave a heave and pushed the bogman against Jack's mother. It was only a little nudge in the stomach, but she caught hold of the rope on the two sides of the gangway and called out: 'Nick, Nick, he hit me.'

The bogman said 'I did not,' dribbling like a babby, and Jack's mother said 'He hit me in the breast.' The way she held on to the two ropes, you would think the bogman was trying to throw her in the River Liffey.

They were now disgraced to the world. People on the boat began to shout things like 'Hit her another belt' and 'Send for the Guards' and 'Eh, missus, give us a dance,' and a gang of women on the quay sang a song called 'Give the Woman in the Bed More Porter'. Jack's da went tearing up the gangway, shouting 'Did you hit that woman?' He was in a roaring rage. He could not get past her to give the bogman a puck of his fist: she was in his way, and when he pulled at her arm to make her let go of the rope she clung on like a conger eel. She was sobbing now: 'Is there no one to protect a harmless poor creature?' His da kept saying: 'Did you hit that woman?' and 'Mag, let go of the rope.'

Jack's mother had made a show of the bogman, and now he was

lepping for fight. He was doing a tap dance on the gangway with his big boots, massacring the air with his fists and wiping his nose with his thumb. He still had a hold of the bottle, and his antrumartins sent the stout gushing out of it in thick foamy spouts over his blue suit. 'Come on,' he said to Jack's da, 'I'm ready for oo. Now oo've met oor match.' The man with him was trying to make peace. 'Mister, nobody is tampering with her. Will you take the decent woman home and let us off the shagging boat?' Jack's da kept shouting: 'Mag, let go.'

Jack wanted to run, run across the bridge and hide in Tara Street station, but there would only be a worse commotion if they thought he was lost. He turned his back on the *Royal Iris* and them and looked at other things: the Customs House, the row of hansom cabs, the lit-up trams on O'Connell Bridge, the Corinthian picture house. He was making himself wonder what picture was on there when a woman bent down to him, a cream-coloured face stooping too low and saying: 'Are you with that lady and gentleman?' He was going to say no; instead he put his fists in his eyes. She pulled one hand down and held a threepenny bit in front of his face. 'Your mammy is only upset,' she said. She wrapped his fist around the threepenny bit. 'Will we wait for them over here?' She led him to the corner of the bridge. It entered his mind that she might be trying to steal him, the way the tinkers on the Barnhill Road would if they caught you, but she looked well-off, so let her.

She was not as old as his mother. 'Will you buy sweets with your threepence?' she asked. He nodded to keep her from annoying him and put his fists back in his eyes. 'What kind of sweets?' He did not think much of her for asking him to belittle his misery with a conversation about sweets; but if ever there was a tomorrow he would buy Scot's Clan: they were his favourites, his mother always bought a bag when they went to the pictures. There was a snot running out of his nose with the crying. The woman took a handkerchief from the pocket of the suit he got last year for his First Holy Communion and wiped his face. A man came out of the crowd; he had a little girl in a harness on his back and a boy by the hand. He was with the woman. The boy looked at Jack as if he had nettles growing out of his ears. 'That's my little boy,' the woman said. 'His name is Cormac. What's your name?' 'Bruce,' Jack said. He thought that Cormac looked a proper little get.

A great jeer went up from the crowd, then there was a grumbling sound like when a concert was over and the clapping had stopped. Then his da came in sight walking quickly, pushing his mother along by the elbow and not minding the people who were looking at them with their eyes out on sticks. His mother's hat was wagging up and down on her head, caught by one hatpin at the back. They looked like Laurel and Hardy, only not funny, with his mother like Hardy in a huff. 'They won't mock and jeer at *me*,' she was saying. 'Bad scran to curs the like of them, may they never have a day's luck.' She made to stop and give a look over her shoulder that would scarify the jeerers, but his da kept pushing her so that while the top half of her was in no hurry the legs were going around like the pedals on a bicycle. You could see that he was raging for having made a show of himself over her.

He stood in their way. Now that they were on the move he did not want them to have to stop and look for him, and maybe call him by his name for the world to hear. When they got close, the woman who had given him the threepence said: 'You're not fit to be in charge of a child. I'm a mother and I – ' His da did not even slow down and look at her. He caught hold of Jack the way a snowball would pick up a stone: it was the sort of thing you could not do a second time if they paid you. He was swept along, and the woman was left with the words hanging out of her mouth while the three of them were off across Butt Bridge like hares.

It was full night, as black as a coal hole, by the time the Dalkey train came in. He kept his eyes fixed on the big advertisement for Ah Bisto on the wall opposite, not looking to right or left in case he might see someone from the *Royal Iris*. His da had walked them to the far end of the platform where there weren't many people, and was cutting up a lump of Bendigo Plug in the palm of his hand and talking to his mother with an air of great sense. Her rage was gone. Now she had a face on her as calm and as put-upon as the Blessed Oliver Plunkett, listening to him with the good nature of a woman being annoyed by an eejit. He was saying sure weren't they all grand and comfortable, owing nothing to no one, and God knows where they might be this time next year, and sure where was the sense in growling and fighting, she was the best woman in the world if only she'd act like a Christian, and hadn't they their health and their strength and wasn't that the main thing? His voice always got a sob in it when he talked about how happy and contented they were: he was so easy to please that Jack's mother would say God pity him if he ever won the Sweep. She gave him a nod or two to keep him happy while he went on at her, and put in the occasional 'Please God' or 'Thank God', like you would respond to a litany.

Jack was taking stock of the day's damage to himself. He decided that by Christmas time it might be safe for him to set foot in Dublin again. This was August. Christmas was nearly half a year away: by then people would have disremembered what he looked like. He saw his mother and himself in Pim's restaurant, sitting down to the two-and-threepenny lunch of turkey and ham that was their treat in between his two visits to Santy: one in Pim's and the other in Switzer's. Last year in Pim's there had been a journey in a submarine: you sat on a bench and watched the fishes and King Neptune go past the windows, then went out by another door and walked along the bottom of the sea to Davy Jones's Locker where Santy was. In Pim's and Switzer's he was a man, not a mott with red crayon on her nose, like in Woolworth's in Dun Laoghaire. He sat in a cave made of sugar bags, shook hands with you with his glove on, tore your ticket in two and hooshed you through a curtain and back into the shop with your present wrapped in blue paper. It was very good for a shilling.

In the restaurant high on the balcony there was the minty smell of tablecloths and the heavy silvery look of the menu holder and the pepper and salt cellars. You put your parcel under your chair for a start, then had a dekko through the twirly iron of the railing at the counters below, black with people. It would put you in mind of a bazaar in the Fitzpatrick *Traveltalks*. The little wooden cups with money and dockets in them went criss-crossing the shop on wires, like baby trams: high up, but not so high as you were. Your mother told you to sit still: 'You have a bee in you.' The waitress brought the plates of celery soup. Celery was disgusting, but here you did not look down your nose at it: this was not home, but Pim's; this was not called your dinner, but your lunch; this was Christmas, and you would die as soon as waste a drop of it. You let your spoon, weighing a ton and as deep as a cup, lie on the bottom of the plate so that the soup stood above the rim for a moment, then softly, thickly, flooded it.

He thought of next Christmas, remembering the tickling celery

26

smell that made your nose weep. As he saw himself lifting the first spoonful, a voice cried out, sharp as a splinter: 'That's the woman and the boy off the *Royal Iris*,' and there at the next table were the woman who had given him the threepenny bit and her little get of a young lad, Cormac. Cormac was pointing at him. People in the restaurant gawked. He felt the shame rising in his face like purple ink and tried to tug his mind out of Pim's and back into Tara Street station. While he was telling himself it was only a fancy, his curiosity dawdled and he saw the faceless manager of Pim's come marching up through the gapers, saying in a voice that shook the sprig of holly on the table: 'Is that the drunk woman who was on the *Royal Iris?*' Even the shoppers down below went quiet as he buried his face and his shame in the celery soup.

He stood hating with all his heart the eejity smiles of the two young ones on the advertisement for Ah Bisto. When the train roared in his da was saying that sure when all was said and done weren't they as happy as Larry.

The train was full on account of the bank holiday. In the next compartment, behind the framed picture of the Rock of Cashel, a man was singing:

> 'Oh, says your old wan to my old wan,
> Will you come to the Waxies' Dargle?
> And says my old wan to your old wan,
> Sure I haven't got a farthing.'

Squeezed between his mother and the window, he did a silent recitation of the twelve stations to home, the stations of his cross: Westland Row, Lansdowne Road, Sandymount Halt, Sydney Parade, Booterstown, Blackrock, Seapoint, Salthill, Dun Laoghaire, Sandycove, Glenageary and, finally, Dalkey and the quick half-run, like robbers, along the dark side of Sorrento Road and into the safety of Kalafat Lane. She would start a row tonight as soon as the front door was shut and the gas lit. He would back-answer her and the day would end with a slap and the hard feel of her ring: but at least at home no one save himself would know. He took *Film Fun* from the pocket of his raincoat and read Charlie Chase, the eye in the back of his head keeping count of the stations. If only she would stay quiet for a half hour he would be on the pig's back.

Along by Merrion you could see into the lit-up kitchens of houses where the quality lived. Then a roar and a sight of white gates, and the train was keeping the main road company, racing a tram past the convent where his da's sister, Sister Mary Gonzales, had died. His da and his mother blessed themself as the convent went by. He had seen only one dead person in his life: that was Biddy Byrne in her coffin. They had lifted him up one November night when he was five, and instead of her face he had seen a mask. It was the face of Our Lord, the dark blotting-paper face that was left on the towel owned by your woman, St Veronica. No one had told him why. Was the face of the corpse too terrible to be seen without a mask? It was, of course: for if the sight of the mask itself froze his heart, what must the face be like? It haunted him forever afterwards, the mask with the face behind it: it hung over his shoulder and looked at him out of mirrors, it waited for him in dark rooms and in the backyard at night, it was behind the yellowy lace curtains of the house where Biddy Byrne had lain coffined. He began to fear other things: how the eyes in the picture of the Blessed Virgin followed him around the room, and how, in Lent, the covered-up statues in the chapel shifted under their purple cloths. He had not seen a corpse since Biddy Byrne and time enough if he never saw another one.

At Blackrock three people got out. His mother had been as good as gold since Tara Street, not opening her mouth to say yes, aye or no. The granny knot in his stomach began to loosen, and as the train slid towards Seapoint he turned from Charlie Chase to Sidney Howard, the Whimsical Wag. It was as if he had let go his grip on a leash, for, on the instant, his mother remarked 'Wasn't it a glorious day?' to two girls sitting opposite.

He put his forehead against the cold glass of the window. He could see the girls' reflection. 'Gorgeous,' one of them said, delighted to be spoken to by a respectable married woman. The other one, thin as a lath and sunburned, said: 'We were in the Phoenix Park.' From the full-of-herself way she said it you would think they had been to England.

'Wasn't that grand for yous,' his mother said. 'Were yous at the a-zoo?'

At this the thin one looked humble and ground her bum onto the seat. 'No, only the Furry Glen.' The other one, with thick legs that got even wider as they went up, put on a bold face and said: 'Sure, you'd get sick of the old a-zoo.' She had a stuck-on beauty spot on her chin and was a tooth short at the side. The pair of them knew that the Furry Glen was not a patch on the zoo.

His mother was kindness itself. 'And what would yous go near the a-zoo for?' she said, as if only scruff from the slums would set foot in it. Then having put butter on their bread, she put jam on the butter. 'The Furry Glen? Oh, how well yous went to the right place.' You could see that the compliment put great heart into the girls.

'Were we ever in the Furry Glen, Mag?' his da said, trying to remember.

'We were never out of it,' she said, taking him up short. Jack knew by the dare in her voice that she had never been in the Furry Glen, wherever it was, in her puff. 'Don't mind him,' she said to the girls. She was as grand as the quality at Christmas.

The girls were all smiles and politeness, not knowing that she had a sup taken. He longed for them to get off at Seapoint, but by the look of them and the way they talked he knew they lived in a place like the Tivoli, below Sandycove. The Tivoli was two buildings with iron stairs on the outsides and balconies with clothes hanging over them to dry, like bunting during the Eucharistic Congress. Rough people lived there. The girls would only get out at Seapoint if they were maids for well-off people, and they were not, on account of maids always had country accents.

The one with the thick legs looked at him. 'Is that your young lad, missus?' she asked. He hid behind *Film Fun*.

His da said with a laugh: 'Oh, that's Jack. Aren't you, son?'

His mother told him to answer people when he was spoken to. The one with the sunburn said: 'The creature. Ah, he's shy.'

'Divil a shy,' his mother said. 'I said, put down that comic.'

She made to tug it down from in front of him and the page tore across. She looked at the comic as if it had torn itself on purpose to make a fool of her. The sunburned one said: 'Ah, his comic.' Then, before he could help it, he let his mother know with his eyes that it was her fault and the fault of the drink. It would surprise you how quick she could be on the uptake: in an instant the good humour was gone and her look bored into him. He was a sleeveen, she was telling him, for having turned against her. She grabbed the comic out of his hands.

'There,' she said to the girls, 'that's the thanks you get. You take them out of Holles Street Hospital when their own didn't want them, and at the end of the road they'd hang you. You slave for them, and for what? Me good neighbours, me own mother, they warned me. "He'll turn on you," they said. "He's a nurse-child, you don't know where he was got or how he was got, you'll rue the day." And sign's on it, their words has come true.'

She nodded at her own foolishness. The two girls gawked at her. He heard his da say with a growl: 'Ah, not at all.'

They were coming into Seapoint. He wiped his eyes with his sleeve.

'You do your best for them,' she said, 'and they'd stab you. Dr Enright said to me: "You'll never rear that child, ma'am," he said, "he's delicate." But I did rear him and he wanted for nothing. He ought to go down on his bended –' She stopped. Then he heard her say in a new voice, her looking-for fight voice: 'Is something up?'

He knew without seeing it that one of the girls had grinned or given the other one a nudge and she had noticed it.

'I said, is something up?'

The one with the thick legs said 'No.' He looked and saw that her face was red.

'Make a jeer of someone else, don't make a jeer of me,' his mother said. 'Pair of faggots.'

'Ah, shush now,' his da said.

'I won't shush,' she said, a scream in her voice. 'Don't tell me to shush. They won't snigger at me, yella-faced rips the like of them.'

The buffers slammed and there was a gasp of steam. A man called out 'Seapoint!' Without a word, the two girls were on their feet and out of the compartment like whippets, the one with thick legs beginning to wail like a banshee. The door hung open after them; there was a banging of carriage doors and a gas lamp hissed on the platform. 'The divil's cure to them,' his mother said. He wondered if they had got back into the train further along.

He took back the comic without her noticing. Time enough for a cry when he was safe at home.

Chapter 3

The town is fashionable now. There are boutiques and smart pubs. Last night I looked up at Dalkey Hill and saw the yellow porch lights of a score of cantilevered bungalows, whereas in the past there was pitch blackness. The hill was where people lived, they would tell you, who ate their young: wild tinkerish families in decrepit cottages at the foot of the quarry. A third of the hill had been gouged out and carried off on the Atmospheric Railway to make the mile-long granite piers at Dun Laoghaire, leaving an amphitheatre of sheer granite cliffs with a ruined castle perched on the very edge. From the castle in those days, one saw fields sloping half-way down to the town, and there the big houses began. One of these was Enderley, where my father worked as a gardener. The house still stands, but it was sold to Catholics, who changed the name to Santa Maria.

My father began work there in 1898 when he was fourteen, at ten shillings a week. Coincidentally, he received that same amount as his pension when he retired, fifty-four years later. He worked for the Jacobs, who were Quakers and biscuit manufacturers, and their garden was as steep as a goat track and consisted of lawns, front and rear, a tennis court, an orchard, a rose garden, a meadow, an acre of vegetables and a dank pond, grandiosely referred to as 'the lake'. There were, in addition, greenhouses, stables and chicken coops. Aided by the under-gardener, Jack O'Reilly, my father raked the gravel paths, scythed and saved the meadow-grass, built rockeries, harvested the fruit, fed the poultry and collected the eggs, Sundays included, pruned the rose trees, weeded the flowerbeds, planted, watered and fertilized, cleaned the pond, trimmed the hedges, swept leaves, rolled and mowed the lawns and tennis court, cut back the tentacles of creepers, dug vegetables for each day's dinner and chopped logs for the fires. On Sunday mornings, besides attending to the poultry, he washed and polished the Daimler in which the

Jacobs were driven to Meeting by – surprisingly for the early 1900s – a chauffeuse, with the intriguing name of Miss Grubb. It was, he would tell his friends at that harbour wall, the best job in the country. Each Christmas Eve, he would be summoned to the pantry to receive a handshake from Mr Jacob, at whose elbow stood Miss Grubb, ready to present him with a pound note, a tin of biscuits and a tumbler of Irish whiskey. He was unused to any drink stronger than a bottle of stout at weddings or funerals, and the whiskey made him garrulous and restless. He would come home, thrust the money at my mother with the grandeur of a nabob, sit, jump from the chair and announce with a sob in his throat that old Charlie Jacob – who was his senior by five years – was the decentest man that ever trod shoe leather. Then he would say: 'Show us that pound note again, Mag,' and look at it as if it were the last ever to be printed. To him, ten hours' toil each day was as natural as shafts to a dray-horse. The Jacobs were not only quality, they were his family.

I met Mr Jacob only once: on the steps by the tennis court. A grave figure with a George V beard reminded me that it was with the right hand, not the left, that one shook hands and gave me a wafer biscuit while my father looked on, weak with pride. Afterwards, I was made to feel that a lay version of the Holy Ghost had descended on me, and but for my promptitude in eating the biscuit it would almost certainly have been commandeered and borne home to my mother as a sacred relic.

One day my father was sent on an errand from which there was a ha'penny change. He was embarrassed to disturb Mr Jacob for the sake of what was, even in those days, an amount not worth mentioning, so he simply pocketed the coin and forgot about it. At going-home time he was summoned to the library where his employer was seated in a leather armchair, making a church steeple of his fingers. He said: 'Keyes, where is my halfpenny change?' My father blushed like a thief caught red-handed. He fumbled in his pocket for the ha'penny and began to stammer. Mr Jacob cut him short. 'Keyes, half-pennies make shillings, shillings make pounds, and that is why I am sitting where I am and you are standing where you are.'

My father was delighted to be the recipient of such wisdom. He repeated it at home, at the bookie's and in the middle of bouts of tug-o'-war, always with the coda: 'And begod, wasn't he right?'

Everyone at Enderley worshipped Mr Jacob. In fact, the only dissenting voice was that of the visiting seamstress, a Scotswoman, who would stick her head into the dining-room when the Jacobs were entertaining and hiss: 'One o' these days h'us'll be yous and yous'll be we's.'

When Mr Jacob fell ill and died my father was inconsolable. The pillars of his world had toppled, and for weeks he moped and reneged at whist drives. My mother sat and brooded, not from grief but in fear that Enderley would now be closed up and sold, leaving us as poor as Job's ass. It was not to happen just yet, however. Mrs Jacob had survived her husband and, although afflicted with a worsening heart ailment, refused to be moved to her married daughter's home in Mountmellick. My father continued to receive his wages, and it became one of his extra duties to return to Enderley each evening at eight-thirty and – assisted by Miss Grubb – carry the old lady upstairs in a kind of sedan chair. As Saturday was the chauffeuse's night off, it was arranged that I should deputize for her on that evening, and I was duly posted between the rear shafts of the chair.

Mrs Jacob was corpulent, and I was fifteen: as thin as a lath and not more sturdy; what was worse, I made a speciality of fainting. I had done so, spectacularly, during Benediction in my days as an altar boy, and again while on parade with the sea scouts, landing on the scout-master's cocker spaniel. Following the latter incident, a court martial quite unjustly decided that while my indisposition was genuine the direction of my collapse had been premeditated, and I was stripped of my badges and expelled. The infinitely more terrible consequences of becoming light-headed and losing my grip on the sedan chair kept me awake nights. I had crazed visions of Mrs Jacob tobogganing down the stairs, failing to negotiate the half-landing and shooting over the banisters in a blur of taffeta. In the event I hung on, but just as animals can smell fear, so she sensed mine and squealed with terror during every inch of the ascent. Within a month, she needed only to set eyes on me to realize that it was Saturday again, and would moan piteously: which, in turn, made my palms sweat dangerously. To everyone's relief, it was soon decided to engage a full-time nurse with splendid biceps, and I became redundant. The old lady's daughter, Mrs Pim, asked me one evening if I had a favourite author. Eager to elicit admiration, I lied and said: Shakespeare; whereupon she went into the library and returned with a mildewed copy of the collected plays, which became my total remuneration and retirement pension combined.

The time came when Mrs Jacob took her final journey in the sedan chair. Was it true, I asked my father on the day of the funeral, that they buried Quakers standing up? 'Jasus,' he snarled, distracted by grief, 'do you think they do it sitting down?' Enderley was put up for auction and the new Ireland, represented by a couturière and her schoolteacher husband, carried the day. They would, we were assured, require a gardener: news which my mother took to be the direct result of her colloquies with God. 'I have a great leg of Him,' she said happily.

Mrs Pim dispensed gratuities to the staff. She appeared in the fruit garden while I was assisting my father to loot the loganberries and whatever else the new owners were unlikely to miss, and handed him a cheque for twenty-five pounds. My heart sank, for my mother had reckoned on a hundred at least, and there would be ructions. My father took the cheque with one hand and addressed the forefinger of the other smartly to his forehead; but the Jacobs' bounty was not so easily exhausted. In addition to the lump sum and his pension of ten shillings a week, Mrs Pim wished him to have a keepsake: one of her late father's treasures. It seemed that Mr Jacob had been in San Francisco at the time of the earthquake and in the ruins of a burnt-out jewellery shop had come across thirty or so wire spectacle frames, soldered together by the heat of the fire. Mrs Pim reverently placed the tangle of charred wire in my father's hands and stepped back with an indulgent smile, the better to enjoy his awe. He stared at it in stupefaction: to his credit, he recognized a lifetime's supply of pipe cleaners when he saw them. But a moment later he remembered 'the poor Master': tears came to his eyes and he carried the spectacle frames home to my mother in maudlin pride.

'Mag, look what the master left me!' He shoved them under her nose, adding: 'Them's worth money.' All my father's cygnets were swans, and by now he had convinced himself that the frames were priceless; also, of course, he was anxious to circumvent her fury over the lump sum.

My mother said nothing, but the following day she and the spectacle frames were laughed out of McManus's pawn office. He came home from work to find the fire out and the tea not ready. She had taken to her bed, from where she loudly implored the picture of the Sacred Heart to tell her what evil she had ever done to be chained for life to an old gobshite.

The new owners of Enderley asked my father to act as resident caretaker for two weeks until they moved in. He was delighted: it meant that he could smoke his pipe in the summerhouse as the sun set and view his domain with the eye of a Crusoe. Best of all, he could roam the house at will, tick off tomorrow's runners in the library and sleep like royalty in the master bedroom. My mother watched him set off, with his nightshirt, wrapped in brown paper, under his arm. 'It's well for some,' she said. 'He'll come home tomorrow to persecute us with how soft the bed was and the colour of the curtains and lavender in the pillows. We'll hear nothing else for a month.'

She was mistaken. Next day at breakfast he was oddly quiet. She waited for him to launch into a garrulous account of his night of luxury and, when he said nothing, asked: 'Well, anything strange or startling?'

He gave her a sharp look. 'What'd be strange?'

She said: 'Was the bed comfortable itself?' fetching me a wink.

He looked past her at me. 'I seen Father Creedon in the town, son. He gave me a great salute.'

My mother, snubbed, cut a slice of bread and almost shied it at him. Keep your secrets, her look said. That evening after tea he seemed unwilling to return to Enderley for the night. He dawdled at our gate to argue horses with Terry Dunne, then came back to pick invisible weeds from the cracks in the path. He was the most easygoing man alive, but as the days passed he became edgy and solitary: I even caught him crossing himself, unbidden by my mother, with holy water before leaving the house. Then, when the fortnight had almost run its course, he asked me if I would like to spend the last night with him. In accepting, I was probably too excited at the prospect of sleeping away from home to look for an ulterior motive.

The electricity had been disconnected and we walked through the empty house with flashlamps, ensuring that every door and window was locked, bolted and, often, padlocked. He was conscientious by nature, but by the time he had finished sealing us in for the night no creature larger than a fieldmouse could have found its way in. We retired to the Blue Room at the head of the stairs, he re-testing every locked door on the way. From there one could see the lights of Dublin ten miles away across the arc of the Bay, and by the reflected glow of a street lamp on Cunningham Road outside I could make out my father sitting stiffly upright in the other twin bed. From his attitude he seemed to be listening, but there was no sound except for a dog barking or the chuffing of a train. I asked him something, and he said 'Yis, yis!' impatiently, as if willing me to be quiet.

The strangeness of the bed and the emptiness of the house around us kept me awake until after midnight. I was drifting towards sleep when he reached out, shook me and said 'Whisht!' in a blood-freezing whisper. Someone was coming up the stairs.

It was a soft footstep, like the brushing of a slipper on a carpet. A riser creaked, then there was the gentle padding again. The hairs rose on my neck, my flesh crawled. A floorboard sighed as it came closer. 'It's him again,' my father said, and I knew it was not a burglar.

We heard the sound of a door handle across the landing being turned and released, and I remembered that ours was the only unlocked door in the house. Now I knew that people could really die of fright. My breath would not come. Then whatever or whoever it was started across the landing: an unhurried step, as if from an infirmity. 'God rest all poor souls in Purgatory this night,' my father prayed as the door handle turned.

There was a creak as the door, no longer held, sagged open. With eyes shut, I willed myself to faint and for once could not. The footsteps began again, but were moving away from us now, towards the stairhead. We heard them become fainter, and after perhaps a minute they were gone. I had held my breath for so long that it came out as a moan.

'Now do you believe me?' my father said, forgetting that he had omitted to forewarn me. 'Now am I a liar?'

My shaking almost dismantled the bedstead. When it at last ceased I realized why he had inflicted the ordeal upon me: not selfishly so that I might lessen his own terror by sharing it, but to bear witness. He had heard the same footsteps on each of the preceding nights, and in the morning every door was still locked, every bolt secure. It was so on the following morning, and to the end

36

of his life he insisted that we had heard 'old Charlie Jacob' bidding farewell to the house.

No one ever believed us except the kind of people who swore by banshees and death knocks, and I was at that uppish age when I despised them for swallowing a story which, in their place, I would have scoffed at. The fact that it did happen still rankles.

At the age of sixteen my mother was walking out with a lad named Ernie who was a crew member of a B and I vessel sailing between Dublin and Liverpool. To Ernie's misfortune, my father set eyes on her in the town and at once proposed: not to her, but to her parents. It was the age of 'made' marriages, and considering his total lack of coherent utterance on the occasions when it was most necessary, it is a wonder that he ever made a case for himself.

On the debit side, his family came from Ballybrack two miles away, which was then a mere crossroads, and so were looked upon in Dalkey as runners-in. Also, they lived in one of the dilapidated thatched cabins at the foot of the quarry cliffs. No class is as snobbish as the very poor: the less they have, the more it counts for, and my mother's family, the Doyles, boasted that they had been in Dalkey for two generations and lived on Sorrento Road, not a stone's throw from the quality. In my father's favour, however, to work for the Jacobs of Enderley signified a job for life, and – the deciding factor – he had the promise of one of the new red-bricked cottages in the Square. The match was agreed to. My mother's opinion was neither sought nor offered, and if her account is to be believed she accepted her fate with lamb-like docility. 'In those days,' she once told me with a look which was an indictment of my own waywardness, 'you did as you were bid.' And that, for more than forty years at any rate, was the end of Ernie.

She and my father were married in 1905 when she was seventeen and he twenty-one. The Doyles were glad to have one mouth less to feed, and their consciences were clear, for my father was a born provider: his vices were whist drives, Bendigo plug tobacco and a sixpenny bet at the bookie's. He was the kind of man who thanked God for a fine day and kept diplomatically silent when it rained. Or rather, he would look up at the drizzling overcast and say: 'The angels must be peein' again'; and I had an instant mental

37

picture of a group of winged figures standing around a hole in the clouds relieving themselves. He prefaced every weighty pronouncement with 'Do you know what I'm going to tell you?' and every disagreement with a snorted 'What are you talkin' about, or do you know what you're talkin' about?' The only real adventure in his life was the War of Independence, when he and his brother Johnny answered the Call, were issued with a rifle each and for two years marched around a field at weekends.

As far as Dalkey was concerned, the war might as well have been in Pago-Pago: in fact it was my uncle Johnny who gave the town its one hour of excitement. One evening, rather than return home from arms drill along unfrequented backroads as ordered, he appeared in Castle Street dragging his rifle behind him, apathetic and uncaring. Turning into McDonagh's pub for a pint, he found it to be full of policemen who, while they often turned a blind eye to a group of armed guerrillas playing pitch-and-toss in a cow pasture, could not and would not tolerate *lèse-majesté*. Johnny was arrested and placed in a cell to await a military escort, which, since possession of firearms was a capital offence, would probably serve as his firing squad also. In due time he found himself being marched along Ulverton Road with three armed Black and Tans in front, three behind and one on either side. Meanwhile, news of his capture had spread and his comrades had been alerted, with the exception of my father who, incommunicado, was feeding the hens above at the Jacobs'.

As prisoner and escort were passing an outcrop of jagged rocks known as the Green Bank, shots rang out. The Tans scattered and took cover in front gardens, onlookers threw themselves face down, and Johnny was left standing in the middle of the tram lines. There were shouts from the Green Bank of 'Run, Johnny!'

The Keyes family were all as stubborn as jennets: like dreams, they went by contraries. 'Who's there?' Johnny wanted to know.

An agonized voice roared: 'Us, us!' and an answering fire from the Tans went screaming against the granite rocks.

'Who's us?' Johnny demanded, not giving an inch.

Oats Nolan's head appeared through a cleft, like a blood-red sun. 'Me, for Jasus' sake. Will you run?'

With bullets snapping at his boots, Johnny ran. He ran all the way to Dun Laoghaire, where his sister Nellie later met him with a suitcase and a pound note. and that evening he caught the mailboat to Holyhead and ended his days working happily in Preston.

The incident brought his relatives under suspicion. and one morning my mother sat up in bed. released the window blind and saw a man standing on the wall of the back yard. He wore a black jacket and tan trousers and was pointing a Lee Enfield at her. She had barely time to say 'Ojesusmaryandjoseph!' when the front door was smashed in and my father was dragged out of bed and slammed against the wall. wearing only the old shirt he slept in.

The raiding party was looking for guns. and my father swore black was white that he had never seen a gun, much less owned one, in his life. Before my mother was half-way through the Prayers for the Dying, the Tans had pulled up floorboards, bayonetted the horsehair sofa and ransacked the wardrobe. A rifle muzzle swivelled towards her.

'Oo said you could stay in bed? Come on. Sleeping Beauty: git aaht of it!'

She had set one shaking foot on the floor when a young officer walked in. He saluted her courteously, begged her to remain where she was. rebuked the Black and Tan for his unmannerliness, and proceeded to take charge of the search. My mother prayed and keened, while my father strove to achieve the impossibility of keeping his hands raised, as ordered, and the front of his shirt down. The Tans combed the two rooms, the yard, the coal shed and the ivy-smothered privy. then the officer saluted again, stroked his pale moustache as he apologized to my mother for the intrusion, and departed with his men.

When tea and time had restored her senses, she laid it down as holy writ that the young officer was the thoroughest gentleman you could meet in a year's walk. Her high opinion of him was even further enhanced when my father confessed that there were two rifles under the mattress on which she slept and that they probably owed their lives to Sandhurst chivalry.

In every relationship there is the lover and the loved. and the loved has the upper hand. So it was my mother who called the tune. I doubt if she ever thought of my father romantically. Hard times had much to do with it, and also perhaps the arranged marriage. As well. there is in the Irish a reserve which is masked behind the boisterousness. We bleed, but not from the arteries. We like the sentimentality of old songs because we confuse loose tear ducts with soft hearts. A blunt declaration of affection is an excuse for a piece of stock repartee: to accept it on its own terms would be to expose oneself irretrievably. Also, in my parents' time and class it was presumptuous even to *think* romantically: that was for the quality and the people in books.

They had several children, all stillborn. On the last occasion, my mother was operated on and her life despaired of. My father was fond of reliving the darkest moment: ' "Keyes," says the doctor to me, "will you go home to hell out of that and let the woman die in peace!" ' And he would gesture, as if astonished by his own dexterity in producing my mother alive and well in front of his listeners, while her own nod of corroboration was at once a testimony to her miraculous survival and a dark intimation, which modesty forbade her to put into words, of the agonies she had endured.

For many years I regarded my father as capable of no emotion more complex than, say, his transports of delight when a horse called Battleship won him ten pounds in a pub sweepstake. The distance between his image of himself and the actuality made him seem comical: an impression which probably stemmed from my first memory of him. He had won a Christmas turkey in a whist drive and went to the town hall to collect it. We stood with several neighbours at the end of our lane, awaiting the great moment when he would round the corner of the Barrack Road with a plucked sixteen-pounder under his arm. When he did appear, he was birdless and running as if for his life. What we could not see at that distance was that he was holding on to a piece of string, but a moment later there came into view a very live and infuriated turkey which was tethered to the other end of it and had chased him all the way from the town hall. When he saw us staring, he stopped, whirled around and aimed a vicious kick at it. The turkey dodged his boot, hopping from one leg to the other like a shadow-boxer until his back was again turned, then flew into the air and sank its claws into his leg and its beak into his behind. Old Mrs Quirk, who was watching, tried out of pity for him to pretend that he was fool-acting for our benefit. 'Oh,' she said to me, 'your da is a comical man.'

I was in my late teens and he was sixty-three before I learned otherwise. It was a Thursday, the day my mother went shopping at Lipton's in Dun Laoghaire, then saw whatever film was on at the

40

picture house, and was home by six. That hour was the heart of the day. The Angelus rang and my father would say 'Glory be to Dan O'Connell.' The table was laid under the single light bulb, sausages and white pudding sizzled, I either read my library book or refined my designs, never realized, on the virtue of Nora Kennefick, while my mother darted between the scullery and the range and the range and the table. Today, however, she was late. At six-fifteen my father began to grumble and by the half past was sure she was under the wheels of a bus. The kitchen seemed emptier and greyer with every moment. My own secret fear was that she had met a crony and been cajoled into a snug. It was seldom now that she yielded to her weakness, but if it happened there would be weeks of rows and black looks and Baby Powers bought on tick and smuggled in by neighbours; she would have wild crying fits and pound the walls, and it would end with the horrors and illness; she would either lie in bed for a week with her insides on fire, or hobble about the house, not asking for pity but becoming sullen if she thought it was withheld.

But not today. We had moved by then from the cottage in Kalafat Lane to a corporation house in St Begnet's Villas, and at twenty to seven there was the squeak of the gate and she sailed in, humming to herself, which was unheard of, and in the height of good humour.

The world was back on its feet. 'We thought you were lost,' my father said.

We might as well have not been there. Still humming, she set down her shopping bag, undid the blue inside strings of her coat and took off her hat, lifting it like a chalice.

'The young lad's stomach is roaring with the hunger,' he said, artfully implying that any fault-finding came from me and not himself. Then, as she made no reply: 'It's seldom we hear a song out of you.'

'I ought to cry to suit yous,' she said airily.

She looked at us with a sly half-smile. At once we knew the sign: she was bursting with news and would make the most of it, obliging us to coax it from her in dribs and drabs. You did not ask her straight out: that cost you the game. You feigned indifference, teasing at the secret as if it were a cord lost in the waistband of a skirt.

My father began paring his plug of Bendigo and led off with a low card. 'Was the picture any good itself?'

'Ah, an old love thing, all codology. A body couldn't make head nor tail of it.' She began to lay the table, not minding him.

He switched suits. 'Your horse was down the field today.'

'Was it?' This with an air of total unconcern. 'The going was too soft.'

By now, curiosity was eating him alive. Usually, if a film was bad or a horse let her down, her eyes would burn with ill-temper and we would go on tiptoe until the mood lifted. He played a small trump.

'I suppose Dun Laoghaire was packed.'

'Oh, crowds.'

His voice began to have an edge to it. 'Nothing strange or startling, so?'

She said 'Mm' with a high sing-song inflection which could have meant yes or no. He glared at her and chewed one end of his whiskers, then lost his patience and the game. 'Well, either tell us or don't tell us,' he snarled, 'one or the other!'

'I was treated,' she announced, bursting with the grandeur of it, 'to tea and sweet cake at the Royal Marine Hotel.'

We gaped at her and waited.

She told us, making a meal of every word, of how a woman had come up to her in Lipton's, asked if she was not Maggie Doyle-that-was of Dalkey and introduced herself as none other than Gretta Moore out of the Tivoli in Glasthule.

'Gretta Moore?' my father said. 'I don't know her.'

'Ah, you do know her,' my mother said. 'Her that married Ernie Moore from off the B and I.'

At the mention of the name Ernie it was as if my father's face had been sandpapered clean of expression. He became as still as a statue, and as pale.

'He's retired these two years,' she said, and went on, as dawny as a young one home from a dance, to tell how she and Gretta Moore had waltzed into the Royal Marine Hotel and sat, as good as the best of them, among the women with dyed hair and fur coats, and how Gretta had ordered tea for two and sweet cake and the swallow-tail-coated waiter had called them madam and rushed off like a hare to serve them.

'Making a show of yourselves,' my father said in a voice like poison.

'What show?'

42

'High-up people looking on at you.'

She laughed. 'Pity about them!'

'The whole town will have it tomorrow.'

He was staring her out of countenance, his teeth grinding. A vein stood on his temple. She turned her back on him and was describing to me the wateriness of the tea and the scandalous price of it when he said in a voice I had never heard before: 'Ernie Moore is dead these donkey's years.'

She swung back to him. 'What?'

'I know he's dead.'

'How do you know?'

'I know.'

'Oh, do you!' She was amused by his obstinacy. 'Well, I'll soon tell you on Thursday whether he's dead or no.'

'What's Thursday?'

This was her news. A small worn woman of fifty-nine, her hands red from work, streaks of grey in her hair, blushed as if she were sixteen again, then her head came up almost regally. 'I'm invited down for me tea. To the Moores.'

My father rose slowly from his chair, looking at her. Her lips were pressed tightly together as if to contain her excitement. Without warning, he let out a heart-stopping roar, sprang sideways to the table and brought his fist crashing down on it.

'It's him, it's him. Ernie, Ernie, curse-o'-God Ernie!'

She gaped at him as blow after blow made the table dance. The floorboards barked like dogs and the cups went mad on their hooks. 'May he die roaring for a priest. Curse-o'-God Ernie!' His eyes were someone else's, not his, as he turned on her. 'You go, you set one foot in the Tivoli, you look crossways at a whoormaster the like of him, and be Christ I'll get jail for you, do you hear me? I won't leave stick nor stone standing in the kip!'

He stood gasping for breath, then the thought of Ernie drove him wild again. He looked around for something to vent his hatred on, saw the milk jug, snatched it from the table and raised it above his head with the milk dribbling down on him, then he changed his mind about smashing it, put it back on the table, and instead pulled his pipe from his pocket and dashed it against the range. I have the pieces still.

During her life my mother was often dumbfounded, but never for long. Now she came back at him, and the Doyle tongue was heard.

'Look at you, look at the yellow old face of you. The whole town knows you for a madman ... aye, and all belonging to you.'

He began to skip with rage. 'With your ... your cups of tea and your sweet cake and your Royal Marine Hotel.' Then, again: 'Ernie ... Ernie! You'll stay clear of him Thursday and every other day.'

She came towards him swiftly until her face was inches from his. Her words pounded into him like nails.

'Because you know I preferred him over you, and that's what you can't stand. Because I never went with you. Because you know if it wasn't for my father, God forgive him, forcing me to –'

I fled up the lino-covered stairs, away from what was unforgivable to listen to. Her voice followed me: 'You went behind my back to him because you knew I wouldn't have you,' and even through the closed bedroom door I heard her flay him with the betrayals of forty and more years ago. But the real come-uppance was mine, for nothing is more damaging to the self-esteem than when other people break out of their allotted roles as mere appendages to one's own life and usurp the passions we thought were our property. There was a rough scraping noise from downstairs as though the kitchen table had been shoved against, and I heard her say clearly and loudly: 'Go on, do it. And that'll be the first time and the last. I'll leave here if I have to sleep on the footpath.' Then the front door slammed, but it was he who went out. From the window I saw him set off, hatless, and disappear out of the yellow circle cast by the street lamp.

As minutes passed, my feelings of shock and dismay began to be debased by hunger pangs. Then I heard the sound of frying and picked up the courage to go downstairs. She showed no sign of the quarrel: apart from my father's absence, it might not have happened. I started to eat and as she stirred her own tea I saw to my astonishment that she was smiling to herself. I asked her: 'Will you go on Thursday?'

A look of sadness came on her face and I knew she would not. Then the smile came back.

'The jealous old bags,' she said proudly.

Chapter 4

'Put away your copybook,' his da said, 'get up to hell out of that and we'll take the dog for a run around the Vico.'

One day his mother had gone into Dublin and come home dragging the dog behind her with a piece of old rope for a lead. It was a right skinamalink of an object, what with its sides sticking to its ribs, the hairs on its belly gummed together with dirt, straw and bits of sweet papers, and its tail between its legs. The pipe nearly fell out of his da's mouth when he saw it. Fluff, the cat, let out a woeful screech and her fur went up like spikes. The dog made a mad dive under the big bed in the kitchen. 'What is it?' his da said.

'Don't be such a jeer,' his mother said. 'It's a German collie.'

Jack got down on his knees to have a proper dekko at it. He made sucking noises and knew that it had started to wag its tail for he could hear the po being banged against. It was a peculiar conundrum of a dog: it had the back half of a collie, right enough, but the head of one of them alsatians.

'There's not a dog the like of it in Ireland,' his mother said.

'Bejasus, I believe you,' his da said. 'Has it a name to it?'

'Jack,' she said.

His da thought she was codding him. 'Jack!' he said, laughing; then he knew she was in earnest, for the po shot out from under his bed, the dog was so delighted to hear his name called. At this, his da went into a long rigmarole about how wasn't it the price of her to bring home the one dog in the country with the same name as the young lad, and how from now on every time they called the shagging dog the child would answer and every time they called the shagging child the dog would answer.

'Not at all!' his mother said. 'Jack, come here to me.'

And the dog barked and Jack said 'What, mammy?'

'Aren't we nicely handicapped?' his da moaned.

Of course, the softy he was, inside a month he thought the sun

45

shone out of Jack the dog. He brushed and combed him till his coat would throw your reflection back at you and even took him to whist drives to show him off, and sure enough, once the hollows in his sides filled out people would stop on the road to ask what class of an animal was it. His da would say it was easy knowing they had never been to Germany, because that's what it was, a German collie, and the dog would look up at him with a grin on its face. Where or how his mother got the dog they never found out, but one November day, seven years before, she had traipsed into Dublin without a word to his da and came home, not with a dog, but carrying a bundle that turned out to be Jack himself. So he supposed his da was relieved that it was only a dog she had landed him with this time.

He liked the long walk up the Vico with his da and held still while his mother half choked him with his scarf and squeezed the tops of his ears inside his cap. 'Bless yourselves going out,' she said, flicking holy water after them. 'Pair of pagans.'

First they went down Victoria Road to the harbour where he knew his da would stand colloguing with Oats Nolan and Gunger Hammond and the other old lads. They would lean over the wall and look at Dalkey Island as if it had come up out of the sea during the night, instead of having been there these donkey's years, and talk about how strong the tide was and where a drowned man would come up after ten days, supposing he was to fall in off the pier this instant. His da would stand there gostering all night if you let him, so you pulled at his coat and said 'Da .. da, will we go now, da?' until he said to his comrades 'More powers, so,' and made to leave. Then he would say 'Do yous know what I'm going to tell yous?' and march back to them again to argue the toss. It was against his nature to do anything sudden. He would talk a hole in a bucket and you had to drag him backwards away from them, still speechifying.

At last they were off in earnest, with the dog going mad with excitement: past Derrymore, the haunted house, and the People's Park, which was called Dillon's Park after Miss Dillon, who was fat and had whiskers and kept the little hut of a shop at the gate where you bought fizz-bags. This park was a tame place, with nowhere to hide: all short grass and tarred paths until you came to the sea at the bottom, where when the tide was out you caught baby crabs and starfish and little shrimps, see-through like glass, or knocked barnacles off the rocks for bait. Better was Sorrento Park across the road where you could climb or play cowboys with Tommy Kinsella or hide in the tunnels made by the furze. This was the end of Dublin Bay: you walked around the corner of Sorrento Point, and there was the Vico Road and Killiney Bay in front of you, with the mountains tumbling out to the sea: Kattygollagher, the two Sugar Loafs and Bray Head, and the Vale of Shanganagh quiet between you and them. The Vico was steep and twisty. On one side of it there were blue, white and pink houses, high above the road like cliffs, with their windows gawking at the view; on the other side, far down, were the railway line and the sea. They stopped at the lane that led to the Ramparts, which was the Gentlemen's Bathing Place, where in the summer his da would dive in in his pelt, with the dog swimming rings around him and Jack watching from the rocks. The sea and sky were the colour of slates on a roof and over Shanganagh there was smoke, like a daub of blue paint. They heard the soft far-away sighing noise of the sea on Killiney Strand. He had never known his da not to stop here, to look at the mountains, draw in his breath and say: 'Sure isn't it the finest bloody country in the world!'

A little way further on they left the Vico and climbed the Cat's Ladder, a long flight of high broken steps that led up Dalkey Hill. At the top there was a cottage. His da would ask: 'Do you know who lived there, son?' and he had the answer off by heart: 'George Bernard Shaw, da.' He had asked once who George Bernard Shaw was, but the only answer he could get was 'Oh, a comical card!' as if his da was not too sure himself. At the top of the hill was an old castle, a dark place smelling of pooly and number two. His da lifted him up to look over the wall at the edge of the quarry cliffs: with your back to the mountains you could see towns and spires all the way to Dublin at the corner of the bay, and then there was the long thin neck of land with Howth at the end of it like a black dog on a lead. There was yellow in the sky behind the Three-Rock Mountain where the sun had gone. The lighthouse at the end of Dun Laoghaire pier flashed and a lit-up tram groaned up the hill past Bullock. He tried to make out Sorrento Road. His mother would be sitting in front of the fire now, reading a book by Nat Gould and taking a puff at one of his da's old pipes. She thought this was a secret, but he had caught her once hiding the pipe under her apron, and she sat so near to the fire that the ABC was tattooed on her legs from the heat.

His da said 'You're a ton weight,' and put him down, then sat on his hunkers to have a smoke before they set off across the Back Meadow to Dalkey Avenue. They could hear the dog snuffling as he nosed this way and that, following the smell of one rabbit and losing it for another. There was a ship far out in the bay.

'Da, there's a ship. Is that it, da? Is that our ship coming in?'

His da took a squint at it. 'Ah, no, son. That one's going out.'

'Will ours come in tomorrow, da?'

'Begod now, it might.'

Jack sat on the short grass. The earth was as springy as a sofa, and he wrapped his arms around his knees and began to rock, thinking of when they would be rich. 'We'll be on the pig's back then, da, won't we?'

'We won't be far off it.' His da blew a sad reedy note through the stem of his pipe.

'And what'll we do?'

'Do?'

'When we win the Sweep.'

'We won't,' his da said, 'do a shaggin' hand's turn.'

His da had told him how the nurse had once drawn his Sweep ticket out of the drum, and then, bad scran to her, didn't she drop it. Jack had been so vexed at this that he had called the nurse a blooming bitch, and his da had said it was a corner-boy expression and never again to let it cross his lips. Women were different from men, so you had to go easy with them. 'No,' his da said, 'never call a woman by a name like that, not even if she was a right old whoor.'

The tobacco hissed in his da's pipe when he lit it. 'Come here till I show you.'

He led Jack to below the castle. Past the brow of the hill there was a wide ledge of rock where they came to an iron railing around the stump of what had been a cross. It was a grave, for under the cross there was a long flat stone like a lid.

'Do you know where we are now, son?'

'Dalkey Hill, da.'

'Not at all,' his da said. 'In my day this was called Higgins's Hill, and oul' Higgins used to chase us off it and him up on a white horse. He never set foot in church, chapel nor meeting, and signs on it when he died no one would have him and not a prayer was said over him. Here's where he's buried, and that cross wasn't there a month before it was struck be lightning. Sure they say he sold his soul to the Oul' Fella himself.'

'What oul' fella, da?' Jack asked, beginning to shake.

'Him.' His da pointed to the ground and under it. 'Your man. Isn't the print of his hoof on the wall below on the Ardbrugh Road where he tripped in his rush to carry oul' Higgins away with him?'

Jack looked at the sea, as black and flat as marble now, and at the lights of Bray and the obelisk on Killiney Hill: anywhere except at the grave, for fear he might see the slab move and the fingers of old Higgins come poking out. The mountains looked like people watching him and waiting, and the sky was filled with a sound that was not a sound.

'Da, let's go home.'

'What ails you?'

'I'm afraid of oul' Higgins and it's too dark and I want to go home.'

'Sure ghosts won't mind you if you don't mind them.'

'Da ...'

They went down the cracked steps that led to the Back Meadow and past the rabbit wood. He kept his hand in his da's trousers pocket until the hill rose behind them and hid the cross.

'Da, do you know the thing I'm worst afraid of?'

'What's that?'

'Me mother. Not mammy: me real one. Aunt Chris says that when it gets dark she comes and looks in at me through the window.'

'Is that a fact?'

It had been in the back of his mind like a spider and now it came rushing out. 'Yis, and me aunt Chris says she's tall and with a white face and a black coat, and she comes out from Dublin on the tram and she wants me back. And me aunt Chris says it's not true what mammy said to me on the *Royal Iris* about how me mother was on Lambay Island, or what you said when we got home about how she couldn't get a hold of me from there on account of how she had to stay and mind the seagulls for a pound a week and the only food she got to eat was pollack and Horny Cobblers.'

He was puffed from saying it all in one breath. His da stopped without warning, nearly swinging him into the gorse.

49

'Not true?' he said with a fierce look on him. 'Did I ever tell you one word of a lie?'

If Jack did not stand his ground he would find out nothing. 'I don't believe she's on Lambay Island.'

From the way his da chewed his whiskers you would think the weight of the world was on him. 'No,' he said, 'no, she's not there. But that wasn't a lie, son, it was more of a makey-uppy. Because you were too young in them days. You wouldn't have understood.'

'Understood what, da? Where is she?' He was afraid of what he was now old enough to hear. Oh, growing up was a curse.

For a minute his da looked without answering from the dark land to the sea, his head twisting like a bed knob. Then he pointed and said: 'Do you see that flashing light?'

'The Kish lightship, da?'

'Well, that's where she is.'

'On the Kish?'

His da sighed. 'God help her.'

The Kish was seven miles away. In the daytime it was a black pencil mark out where the sea ended; now its yellow eye winked twice at them.

'But what's she doing on the Kish?'

Smoke rolled from his da's pipe. 'She . . . she cooks.'

'For the lightshipmen?'

'Yis.'

'What does she cook?'

A clearing of the throat. 'Ah, pollack, son. Pollack and Horny Cobblers.'

His da lifted him through the broken part of a wall and into the Back Meadow where the long damp grass tugged at them like beggarmen. The wet came in through his boots, but no matter: now he knew the truth instead of that cod of a yarn about Lambay Island. He felt pleased with himself: because you were just a chiselur grown-ups thought you would swallow any old rubbish, but he had shown his da to the differ. In his mind he saw his mother in the kitchen on the Kish, gutting the pollack and putting them in a frying pan for the supper. But she must be a right thick to think you could eat Horny Cobblers: Tommy Kinsella had told him they would poison you.

His da was saying how it was a hash old wind starting up and that they would need a few extra coats on the bed when another worry came to pester him.

'Da ... what if she got off the Kish? What if she's at home now before us and looking through the window?'

It was night now and he could barely make out his da's face against the blackness of the rabbit wood.

'Well, if she is, I'll tell you what we'll do. I'll come up behind her and I'll give her the biggest root up the arse a woman ever got.'

His face burned with delight. 'Will you, da?'

'I will. And bejasus it'll be nothing compared to the root I'll give your aunt Chris!'

He felt a wetness come into his eyes: his da was the best da in the whole of Dalkey. Then he thought of his aunt Chris, who wore stays and walked very straight and slowly with her feet turned out, and saw her rise into the air on the end of his da's boot. He put his hand over his mouth to hold in a snigger, only it burst into a splutter so loud that the dog answered him from the wood.

After a while they were free of the meadow grass that was like a head of tangled hair and the quarry was at their backs as they walked down the Flags to Dalkey Avenue. His da sang:

"St Peter, St Paul and St Patrick
And the pictures that hang on the wall,
I will give you them into the bargain
If you'll marry me daughter at all ..."

When they reached the road there was no singing, for there were street lamps and you would make a show of yourself. He stopped to rub the white spots on his knees where nettles had stung him; a dock leaf would draw the sting, but it was too dark to look for one. He saw his da ahead of him under one of the lamps. A felt hat, dark around the band from sweat, was rammed square on his head and the hobnails in his boots hit the road like hammers. He had a quick, short, stiff-legged walk, with his elbows nudging the air and his pipe cupped in one hand, the stem of it up his sleeve. He was leaning back against the slope of the hill to keep from breaking into a trot. He turned to call to the dog, who knew they were nearly home and was pretending to pee. 'Curse o' God on you for an animal, how much water is in you?'

Jack ran, skipping, to catch up with him. His da's hand around his was as rough as tree bark.

'Da, I love you.'

His father looked at him as if he had a screw loose. 'Certainly you do,' he said. 'Why wouldn't you?' And the three of them went down into the town.

Chapter 5

Our dog, Jack, was anti-clerical. That was the opinion of Mr Quirk who lived next door, but my father clung to the theory that the dog simply detested the colour black: which did not explain why postmen were allowed to pass unmolested, but let a priest or a brace of nuns appear on our road and Jack's mane rose like the quills on a porcupine. In a moment he would be in front of them, a veritable Pétain of a dog, determined that they should not pass. He growled, snarled and bayed at them, his hindquarters in the air, his forelegs flat on the pavement, his teeth inches away from the hem of a robe or the turnup of a trousers leg. His victims were not to know that he was a fraud – the one time he caught a rabbit he tossed the unfortunate animal into the air with his snout, then held it down gently with one paw until to his puzzlement it died of fright – but one look at those slavering jaws must have convinced many a Little Sister of the Poor that her martyrdom was at hand. What made it worse was that he positively fawned on the Protestant minister, whose black suit had a white pin-stripe.

My mother was scandalized. Her neighbour, Mrs Kinsella – whose addiction to malicious gossip and a protruding lower jaw had earned her the nickname of Mary Plock – had hinted that the dog's militant bigotry was symptomatic of a hidden Godlessness in our house. She sat on a flat granite boulder, less seat than throne, outside her front door where nothing escaped her unblinking eye: she could, so my father insisted, see a midge on the Hill of Howth. Whenever Jack bared his fangs at the approach of clerical broadcloth she would suck on a lone sentinel of a tooth and observe with relish: 'The dog didn't learn *that* be hisself!' Once, I made friends with a boy named Stan Slonom, and it was Mary Plock who told me that he was a Jew and it was a sin to talk to him because the Jews had crucified Our Lord.

At last the inevitable happened and Jack picked on the wrong nun. She fetched him a blow between the eyes with her reticule, whereupon he seized her sleeve between his teeth and shook her arm so vigorously from side to side that she seemed to be imparting a blessing to the entire neighbourhood. When she managed, quite literally, to tear herself loose she made straight for the police station, while the dog trotted proudly back to our doorstep, bearing in his jaws the enemy's colours.

My mother feared two kinds of people: the clergy and policemen. The only honourable circumstance in which the former might cross one's threshold was when death was imminent: otherwise their presence signalled your shame to the world, for it proclaimed apostasy, wife-beating, infidelity or a child gone to the bad. A visitation by a policeman was as degrading: a summons for pilfering firewood might be nothing to write home about in the moral sense, but thereafter it was unwise to brandish your respectability at a neighbour. In fact, at your great-grandchild's wedding breakfast sixty years in the future, a guest would be sure to remark on how warm the room was, adding with a leer and a wink: 'But then the family never went short of firewood!' So my mother was shamed twice over to be in trouble with the police as the result of a complaint made by a nun.

The same day at tea time a civic guard came stooping through our front door, which was high enough for an ordinary Christian, but not for him. He was the 'Cat' McDonald, so named because he had once leaped from a ten-foot wall to catch an apple-thief. Later, when I read *Les Misérables*, Javert's face was his. He had pale eyes, with the bluish tint of sun on ice. There was long dark hair on his cheekbones, and he craved to be feared the way other men need to be liked. His children played alone. One night I saw the glint of his peaked cap while I was wheeling an unlit bicycle. At once I hoisted it on my shoulder so that it ceased to be a vehicle, and he stalked me for three miles, whispering threats and insults while I staggered under the weight. But I was younger – perhaps ten – the evening he came to the house.

Another guard would have been red-faced and apologetic, singing hosannas to our world-wide reputation as decent people. The 'Cat' came in with the face of a public hangman, his eyes ransacking the room for a sign of unlawful affluence. My father, who knew him for a gouger who would begrudge you the time of day, stared sullenly at him, the egg yolk dribbling from his spoon on to the sheet of newspaper we used as a tablecloth. My mother, lost to all shame, was doggedly flirtatious: in moments of desperation she believed, like my grandmother, that she could charm songs from a crow. She shoved a chair against Guard McDonald's unyielding knees, declared that he would have a cup of tea with us ('In your hand, just . . . you will, you will!') and implied with a nudge of her eyes that his steeliness was a sham. Only the whiteness of her face showed how afraid she was. The 'Cat' bided his time until her voice became small and ran down like a clockwork toy. When he spoke, the words were baton blows. He was a great man for phrases. We were the custodians of a dangerous animal. A complaint had been lodged. An attack upon the person of a religious. Intimation of prosecution was hereby given. Good day to us.

At the door he turned to regard my father, who was still eyeing him malevolently, the egg yolk now congealed. My mother was cringing piteously, but perhaps the 'Cat' was not content until my father, too, had been brought to heel.

'Listen here to me, my good man.' For some unexplained reason all Irish policemen have bass voices but his could rattle the windows. 'This matter is coming to court. If you want a lenient view to be taken you will destroy that animal without more ado. There is a gun below in the barracks for such purposes and any one of the guards will put a bullet into him. If you'll be guided by my advice it may go easy with you.'

He was a clever one. I knew by my mother's face that she would grab at the straw, and he knew it, too. My father might strut and bluster, but it was she who ruled the roost. Her terror of the law went far deeper than a two-pound fine and our names in the *Evening Herald*: it was an almost primeval fear, beyond argument or reason, akin to the dread evoked by the *terra incognita* on ancient maps, and in a panic she could no more think or behave sanely than rain could fall upwards. As the 'Cat' turned on his heel to leave, he fetched my father a quick pitying glance to let him know who had the upper hand.

In bed that night I heard my parents whispering in the other room. My father sighed 'I dunno' a couple of times, then was silent as she railed on at him. I lifted the window blind and could make out the dog, exiled in disgrace to the back yard. The next day at breakfast time I said: 'You won't kill Jack, mammy, sure you won't?' She was silent, and my father said: 'Not at all. Don't mind her.' Over my Saturday comic I saw her look at him angrily.

I stayed close to the house all that day, not daring to go to the corner for fear I might see the 'Cat' reappear, this time with a gun in his hand. Towards tea time my father was no sooner home from work than I was sent on a message to Toole's shop. Hurrying back, I caught sight of him turning out of our lane and leading the dog by a length of rope tied to his collar, which in itself was unusual because Jack had always been allowed to run free. I knew straight off that the errand was a red herring and that my father was on his way to the harbour to drown the dog.

I know that my parents were not cruel; in fact I often heard my father inveigh against people who got rid of unwanted animals by taking them into the country and losing them. He believed drowning to be a humane death. Call it ignorance, or say that life had hardened him or that he simply lacked the imagination to feel in his mind the panic, the struggle for breath and the bursting of lungs. And out of bull-headedness he would not give the 'Cat' the satisfaction of seeing Jack die with a police bullet in his brain. At any rate, watching him and the dog disappear down Victoria Road towards the sea, I began to bawl, hating my mother and despising my da for his weakness in not defying her. It was in my nature to slouch off in solitary misery, and I would be lying if I pretended, more than thirty years later, to know why I followed my father to the harbour instead, running to catch up and howling as I ran; but what happened there is branded on my mind as if by lightning.

It was October and a gale was roaring in from the north east: the kind of once-in-ten-years gale that in a night turned the beach at the White Rock from fine sand to pebbles. There was a flood tide and the sea itself seemed to come driving into the harbour, surging over the piers, not in waves but in a great maddened swell which boiled around the boats high on the slipway, then retreated for a new onslaught, turning the stone steps into cataracts. A lobster pot, caught by the wind, went bowling along the road. The air was filled with flying leaves and twigs. The sea thundered, and I felt spray on my face all the way along Coliemore Road. There are two piers, one a stub of granite jutting out from the land, the other at a right angle to it. This second pier catches the full force of the sea and there is a protecting wall running the length of its seaward edge. When I reached the top of the slipway, half-blinded by spray, I saw my father crouched beneath the wall. He was holding the dog steady between his knees and tying one end of the rope he had used as a lead around what looked like a concrete building block. I ran towards him along the pier. I cried out, but the wind shouted harder, and before I could reach him he had gathered up the dog and the concrete in his arms and dropped them over the wall into the sea.

I stopped dead a few yards from him. He said afterwards that my wailing was like the moan of a banshee. He was hanging on to the wall to avoid being blown into the harbour, and I have never seen such a stricken look on a human face as when he turned and saw me. The sea roared, white gobs of foam spat around his boots and Dalkey Island was at his back like a sinking ship. Then another green wall of water came rushing in between the piers, and I saw Jack, unbelievably on its crest, his paws flailing like paddle-wheels.

The sea bore him into the harbour like matchwood, threatening to dash him against the pier. Less from bravery than impulse, I started down the steps cut into the granite. My father shouted out 'Jack!', but I never knew whether he meant me or the dog. Unknowingly, I was running down into the trough of the previous wave, and before I had time to be amazed the sea rose from nowhere: it was around my waist, my chest, and then had swallowed me. The steps were no longer under my feet. I opened my mouth to gasp and was breathing sea water. Then I felt a tug, my own heaviness and the agony of being yanked upwards by my hair. I was hauled back up the steps to the accompaniment of a volley of curses and dumped like Monday's washing on the pier. I choked and retched, and the wind knifed through my wet clothes. I was missing a shoe. After a moment I could make out the blurred figure of my father below me on the steps. He was hanging on to an iron mooring ring with one hand and reaching out for the dog with the other, yelling: 'You cur, you whelp, you whoor's melt, will you come here to me!' He stooped to grab him by the collar, an after-wave broke over him, and then the dog was on the steps, scrabbling with his paws to hold on, for the concrete block was still tied to the rope. My father carried it as if it were a bridal train, and cut it loose when they were safely on the pier. He sat in a pool of water from his own clothes and looked at me and the dog, who was shaking himself nonchalantly. His whiskers dripped. His hat was bobbing below us in the harbour. 'Amn't I the misfortunate poor divil,' he moaned, 'with the pair of yous?'

I should have danced for joy at the dog's reprieve, but my wet clothes and chattering teeth kept my delight within bounds. While I turned blue with cold my father took an oar from the boat-house and fished out his hat. Then the three of us set off for home, my one shoe squelching water, his wet trousers snapping like a whip in the wind, the dog leading the way, tail high, with every appearance of having enjoyed his swim. 'She'll murder us', my father said. 'The woman will ate us.' The litany of his woes embraced my missing shoe, our ruined clothes, unavoidable pleurisy for himself, certain consumption for me, and his utter failure to drown the dog. Identifying Jack as the architect of his misfortunes, he snarled: 'I'll learn you to swim with a ton weight of concrete tied to you!', and made a sudden frenzied kick at him. As the dog bounded effortlessly out of range, my father's sodden boot took leave of his foot and sailed into a garden.

Further up the road, the cup of his mortification brimmed over when we met our neighbour, Tweedy Costello, who kept hens and, in fact, had the beaky profile of a Wyandotte. 'Fine fresh evening,' my father said to him, as if, far from there being aught amiss, it was his daily custom to take a child swimming, fully clothed, in a Force Nine gale. Mr Costello made it a point of pride never to seem astonished, except when there was no reason for astonishment, but on this occasion he turned so sharply to look at us that one of the bicycle clips he wore whether awheel or on foot shot off his ankle and sang in mid-air. My father kept walking, and when our house came into view a moment later he could not have looked more despairing had it been a gibbet.

As soon as he opened the door the dog squirmed past him, through the front room and into the lighted kitchen. We followed him, expecting to hear his survival greeted with shrieks and execrations; instead, we saw my mother on her knees. Tears were streaming down her face and her arms were wrapped around the dog's neck. 'God love him, he came back to me,' she paeaned, while Jack, gratified by his welcome, gave her face a lick and looked around for his supper. 'Ah, he's wet, the creature. Did they try to drown him?' she asked with a fawning shamelessness that made us reel. Her delirium knew no bounds. She fondled his brown head. Then her eyes strayed from him to two spreading pools of water on the linoleum, and she looked up and saw my father and me.

The prosecution never materialized. Perhaps the local sergeant, in whose side the 'Cat' was a long-festering thorn, simply ran his pen through an entry in the summons book, and that was that. Nonetheless, my father bought a muzzle for the dog in a spirit of appeasement, but that canine Houdini managed to escape from it on the first day and chewed it to pieces. He lived, persecuting the clergy, for another nine years.

Our house was Number 3, Kalafat Lane, which was in effect the back entrance to the Pearsons' house. They were a Quaker family who manufactured gates and window frames and regarded us affectionately as their cottagers. The distinction was purely honorary: our actual landlord was a fiery drunkard named Darley, who hung Nazi banners in his front hall and thumped out 'Deutschland Uber Alles' and the 'Horst Wessel Song' on the piano when in his cups. Every Christmas morning, the Pearsons' youngest son, Edwin, who was my own age, would knock at our door and hand in a tin casket of sweets 'for the boy' with a crisp sang-froid which belied his years. My father acknowledged the gift by sending a forefinger in search of a non-existent forelock and becoming incoherent with gratitude. For myself, I envied Edwin his air of self-possession on these occasions, and one year – more in a spirit of slavish mimicry than generosity – I bought three-ha'pence worth of broken chocolate at Da Lundy's shop, wrapped it in a cone of brown paper and duly presented myself at the Pearsons' front door. I asked the parlourmaid if Master Edwin was in, but it was Mr Pearson who came and asked me my business. He accepted my offering graciously, evincing no sign of surprise, nor indeed – as occurred to me years later – gave the slightest indication that he was hearing the first rumble of the revolutionary tumbrils.

Never being one to hide my light under a bushel, I told my parents of my shining deed and awaited the torrent of their praise. My mother was scandalized. We were disgraced; I had gotten Above Myself; it was our role in life to receive bounty, not to dispense it. She looked at me as if I were a changeling and said: 'The brazen impudence of him,' then inquired of the room in general and my father as an afterthought: what was the world coming to? He, being anxious to maintain peace in the house at Christmas time, agreed with her, only to earn one of her black twenty-minute silences by adding frivolously that there were people dying today who had never died before.

Ours was one of a terrace of five two-roomed cottages – my father later built a wooden lean-to scullery at the rear and 'papered' it with pages from a book of oil-cloth samples. The other four cottages were occupied, respectively, by a gentle spinster named Lily Byrne, the sight of whose coffined sister, Biddy, had sent me into screaming hysterics at the age of four; a solitary and lugubrious Protestant named Alf Curtin, whose main diversion was to sit in Dillon's Park and look at the sea with the vague frown of one who was convinced that he had seen it before and was trying to remember where; an elderly couple named Tim and Essie Quirk: he bowler-hatted and with a resident crust of yellow froth on his white moustache which was at once a memorial to the bottle of stout he had had yesterday and a prediction of the bottle he would have today; and the Quinns, who lived in Number 5.

Old Martin Quinn was a tyrant who looked like Bismarck and denounced playing cards as 'the devil's prayer-book'. He had two gipsy-like daughters: Susie who was so vivacious and winning that, remembering her, I still smile, and Maria, the elder, whose swarthiness owed as much to a grudge against soap and water as to pigmentation. Their kitchen was always acrid with smoke, and Maria sat hunched over the fire all day, listless and red-eyed, rarely venturing further abroad than the end of the lane. The fourth Quinn – Johnny – was a year older than I: a spindle-legged, gaunt, amiable dunce with deep catarrh lines under his eyes and skin with the sheen of wax. The old man beat him frequently: usually about the head. Johnny always referred to old Martin as his father and to Susie and Maria as his sisters, and such was the conspiracy of deception practised by adults to keep our minds pure that it was years before we who played with him realized that Maria was his natural mother and the old man his grandfather. Perhaps even Johnny himself did not know; at any rate, it accounted for the beatings and Maria's reluctance to be seen out of doors.

Facing us across the lane was a row of crumbling two-storey

dwellings, soon to be demolished, where my crony, Tommy Kinsella – Mary Plock's youngest – lived. Their next-door neighbour was a crimson-faced man named Redmond who was known to be staunchly pro-British. In the 1930s we were all infected with the rabid nationalism of our parents, who had been 'out' during what was rather grandly called the War of Independence. Old hatreds were virtuously passed on to children, who wolfed them down like sweets. To Tommy's father and mine the patriot dead were gods and De Valera was their pope, and so we would parade with whatever grubby rabble we could muster in front of Mr Redmond's house chanting like pigmy devils:

> 'Red, white and blue,
> The dirty English crew;
> Green, white and yella,
> The brave Irish fella.'

There would be perhaps ten minutes of this before an upstairs window was clawed open and our victim, whose face and bald head were now an awesome mauve, shrieked dementedly that he would swing for us. It was hot air and we knew it. As an anglophile in a den of republicans, he lived on a razor's edge; it would have been a short cut to a Protestant heaven had he raised a finger against cherubs who, God love them, were merely reiterating what the world knew to be gospel truth. As the chanting soared like a *Te Deum* and the false teeth danced in Mr Redmond's head, casual observers remarked on how grand it was to see us away from mischief.

Growing older can be measured by playgrounds. First there was the lane itself, which included a verminous patch of waste ground known as Horner's: a place of weeds, rusting cans and boy-made swamps where, when the sun came out, the earth blazed with broken glass. Here we grubbed for chainies: fragments of earthenware which served as legal tender when we played 'shop' – our games were of a domestic nature, for we were hag-ridden by Teasie Costello, a fearful termagant who stormed like a Valkyrie when thwarted. Once, she announced that six of us would enact a 'play' and bullied the other children into paying an admission fee of a ha'penny each. With fivepence in the box office, which was Teasie's knotted handkerchief, and the audience squatting expectantly among the thistles and pee-in-the-beds, the hapless six were commanded to improvise without benefit of theme or plot. A fathomless silence ensued. We stared dumbly at the spectators, who looked back at us blankly. One of the actors began to bubble at the nostrils, burst into tears, climbed a wall and was gone. The audience became restive and one of the Kavanagh children, whose oriental cast of features had won her the nickname of Anna May Wong, demanded her ha'penny back. At this point I became suddenly inspired. Striking an attitude of outraged hauteur, I pointed dramatically at a corroded flashlight battery lying on the ground and declaimed: 'Who put that bomb there?' In truth, there have been worse opening lines, and I half-expected one of the other actors to seize on it happily. Instead, someone shrieked 'A bomb ... oh, Jasus!', and audience and cast alike – including Teasie Costello – took to their heels, screaming as they fled. I was left alone in the wake of the stampede, and it is small consolation to reflect that I have never since written a line of dialogue half as effective as my first.

In time, Teasie's autocracy was overthrown and the liberated males graduated to Sorrento Park: a paradise of bloody knees, with crags and canyons, grass to wrestle in, slopes to roll down, mortally wounded, and a roofless bandstand which was an outlaws' hide-out, a raft, an airplane, a fort, but never a bandstand. There was also a promenade where in summer my mother sat with the old ones from our road, facing the sea with the gorse yellow at their backs, and conversing of funerals, achieved or imminent. In those days, such is the blur of time, there seemed to be a death in the town every week. There were tragedies, as when a girl I knew was suffocated by sand on the White Rock beach and when Jackie Foley's father was found decapitated in the railway tunnel; but it was usually the old who died. Their passing did not touch us; you went quickly past the house with the drawn blinds and crape on the door, and you walked three steps with the hearse it if passed you on its way to Dean's Grange; but there was no awareness that a generation was quietly fading from view, while your parents, and you behind them, inched forward in the queue. The dead were less real to you than was Tommy Kinsella as a counterfeit Johnny Mack Brown spurring an invisible mount through the furze-cactus of Sorrento Park in a re-enactment of Episode One of *Covered Wagon Days* and uttering the only possible reply to a warning of danger ahead: 'Mister, that's a chance I gotta take.'

We never spoke of villains and heroes: we called them the Bully and the Chap, and at the Picture House on Sunday afternoons the fourpennies were a bedlam of squeals and adjurations to 'Come on, the Chap!' In our games I precociously preferred to be the Bully: not from an inverted élitism, but because in fights I could kick, gouge and pull hair to my heart's content, with the excuse that I was conscientiously trying to behave in character. And Bullies had a supreme advantage denied to Chaps: they could die, exquisitely, with gasps, grimaces, spasms, contortions and infinite variations on how they bit the dust, ranging from thudding face downward to a fastidiously graceful swoon. I even became a connoisseur of cinematic villainy, so that my characterizations ranged through a superb and limitless rogues' gallery. There was the scar-faced and leather-gloved Dick Curtis whom Charles Starrett as the Durango Kid gunned down in one film and who, to my mother's bemusement, rose from the grave like a vampire for the next; Morris Ankrum, a black-suited compendium of jaded corruption; Alan Bridge, whose sour gloominess suggested that he knew in advance how his schemes and himself would meet a dusty end; Walter Miller, a shifty-eyed whited sepulchre, adroit at murdering the girl's father; Kenneth McDonald, the town banker, whom a child would not trust to mind a caramel; and the hirelings: John Merton, Roy Barcroft (a thug incarnate) and Charles King, fat, unshaven and invariably called 'Blackie'. My favourite of them all was Douglas Dumbrille, a suave, smiling, tar-hearted blackguard, who enjoyed his perfidiousness so hugely that the Chap's retributive bullet came too late to point any useful moral.

A year ago I recognized one of my Bullies in the seat next to mine over the Atlantic. He was as menacing and as evil-looking as ever, and I almost wept when he told me he is now a minister and has founded his own thriving church outside Dallas. He sends me his sermons.

After the park came our final playground: the Fields. These were acres of flat grazing land stretching from the edge of the town to the red-bricked Edwardian villas at Castlepark, with not a butte, gulch or mesa in sight; but by then we had abandoned the range for the seedier pleasures of the saloon. Crouched in the lee of hedges or hidden by the tall reeds in the ditches, we played pontoon for cigarette cards and celebrated our emergent manhood by using curses for punctuation and passing from hand to hand a half bottle of flat, stale stout.

The event which lent the Fields a glory of sorts happened during the war – known officially in Ireland as the Emergency. A clerk in the labour exchange had astonished my uncle Sonny by presenting him with temporary work as a nightwatchman. (Sonny was a man of principle: it was not the job itself to which he took exception – *that* meant simply that he was obliged to sleep sitting up in the open air instead of full-length in his bed – but the philistinism which saw no sanctity in the life of meditation to which he had devoutly pledged himself since boyhood.) Early one morning he was limping homeward from his labours through Castle Street when he heard the clatter of hooves behind him. He turned and saw, not the expected straying horse or donkey, but a large deer with a magnificent spread of antlers. Their alarm was mutual: the deer reared and fled the way it had come, encouraged by Sonny's bellow of fear and his attempt to crash bodily through the locked door of the Baby Linen shop.

Public opinion at first ascribed my uncle's graphic account of the incident to a surfeit of the Power's Gold Label he favoured as a sleeping-draught – only a few nights previously he had slept soundly while a group of ruffians carried his watchman's hut, with him inside it, into the old graveyard, where he awoke at dawn surrounded by headstones and marble angels. But there was corroboration: first from Mammy Reilly, who kept the newspaper shop; then from Jack Waldron, who had seen the deer bounding across the Fields and scattering the cows. By mid-morning we knew that it had escaped from the Phoenix Park twelve miles away. The deer herds there had grown to the point where they were starving for want of fodder, and the Government had assigned army marksmen to thin them out.

That a deer should have elected to make a run for it in the interests of self-preservation was hardly remarkable. But in our town they would argue a hole in a pot, and there was heated debate as to why this one had turned its back on the open country just north of the park and instead had crossed the city and the entire borough of Dun Laoghaire at dead of night. Controversy raged. Sonny, who by virtue of his experience had become an authority on the habits of the red deer, held that the animal was simply as thick as a double ditch and had lost its way. My father, citing the homing instincts of tom cats, argued that the psychic powers of animals were beyond human divination and that the deer was making for the sanctuary of Powerscourt Demesne in Co. Wicklow, where his kind roamed freely.

That day after school the deer hunt began. More than a hundred of us – for the news had spread to Glasthule and Sallynoggin – swarmed into the Fields armed with sticks and hurleys, and none had the vaguest notion of what to do if we actually sighted the deer. The chase itself was the thing. It was a raw winter's day, and the passage of cattle through the gaps in the hedges had left pathways of churned-up mud. We ran, cheered and waved our sticks like cavalry sabres, ignoring the probability that our quarry was by now in Castlepark Woods, which were not only private but cut off from us by a high wall.

I have never been physically inclined, and as usual I lagged behind. It was getting dark and I had stepped in a cow flop, and with the best will in the world it is impossible to run gaily and fast when one's boot is enveloped in dung. I stopped near a hedge and began pulling up tufts of coarse grass with which to wipe my boot. The others were far off by now and the sky threw back their war cries. In moments of boredom I have a strong homing instinct, and I had half-decided to sneak off when something made me look up. There, not at the far side of the hedge but from its very middle, the deer was observing me.

My heart almost stopped from shock and fright. There was vapour coming from its nostrils; it made a faint snoring noise. Then I saw its eyes, huge, soft and brown. I had never seen anything so beautiful or so infinitely sad. We stared at each other; there was a tremor, a sudden whirring of briars, and the deer soared clear over my head. It landed with hardly a sound, head tossing as it gored the air with its antlers and ran off towards the woods. All at once it was *my* deer. I gave chase until it vanished, cheering it on and making leaps of my own in delight. Next day, news came that it had been seen in the early hours, high-stepping it along the Bray road past Shankhill, and that was the last of it; so perhaps my father had been right for once and its destination was the deer park at Powerscourt.

Two years later a road was cut through the Fields, and side roads grew from it like shoots. Corporation houses went up – none with a bathroom, for officialdom held that a combination of cleanliness and Irishness was somehow unnatural – and we moved into ʼne of them. Today, the only green spaces are pocket-handkerchief gardens and a sloping football pitch fronted by a sports stadium. Not long ago I was asked to open a fashion show in the stadium. There was an audience of six hundred, and among them I recognized faces I had not seen in a third of a century. Then they had belonged to urchins like myself; now they were light-years away from the dinginess and the scrimping: they drove cars, played bridge and had been to Spain in August. From the relative luxury of their present world they could afford to look back with an affectionate longing for the one from which they had escaped. The high point of that evening was a display of swimsuits, wispy nightdresses and *couture* as *haute* as one would find the length of Grafton Street. A few whoops of mock horror went up – this was, after all, Dalkey. But I thought of my mother in the kitchen of our house not fifty yards away, and for a moment she was alive again and looking out of the back window and through the stadium wall, and I heard her again asking my father what the world was coming to.

Chapter 6

He knew without opening his eyes that it was Sunday: the sounds of footsteps on the road outside were different: quicker and yet quieter. His mother had been to the Women's Mass at nine o'clock, and now his father was dressed and ready for the half-ten: shaved and wearing his blue suit with the watch-chain that had no watch at the end of it, his corns pared from the night before and his black boots squeaking.

Jack was up and washed by the time the first bell went, and took his good suit from the wardrobe, dawdling to have a squint inside one of the three cardboard boxes that held their gas masks. 'That's the end of us,' his mother had sighed the day the boxes were handed out at the town hall, and his da had said: 'Oh, neither dog nor divil will escape this time,' and laughed as if he could not wait to be blown sky-high. There had been screeds in the *Sunday Pictorial* about how when the war came all the children would be what they called evacuated to the country. 'Will I go, too, ma?' he had asked, half-wanting to. 'No,' his mother said, putting on her saint's face, 'we'll die together.' But the war had not happened, and here it was, another year gone, and dust on the cardboard boxes.

The minute his father had his Sunday clothes on, it was as if the house was on fire. Jack's way of eating his breakfast was to spread his white pudding on his bread and make a sandwich. It took time, and his father would groan: 'Can you not eat like a Christian? The priest has the Mass half said.' He lived in mortal dread of being late. He was the first at whist drives and in the queue for the pictures, and would give daggers' looks at the people who streeled in after him and they still in tucks of time. 'Them and their hopping and skipping and slouching,' he would say, 'it's not worth their time to come at all.'

'Sit down and let the child eat his breakfast,' Jack's mother barked at him. He sat, then craned his neck to see how much tea was still in

Jack's cup, and then his head went around in circles, following the bit of bread that mopped up the gravy. The instant the quarter-to bell went there was no holding him. He roared: 'Am I to damn me soul over you?' and flung open the front door. And with tea scalding his mouth, Jack followed him out.

The first person they met that Sunday was Tish Meredith. There was a mystery about Tish. She wore a beret on the side of her head and ear-rings the size of the hoops you threw at the Hoop-la when the fête came to Dun Laoghaire, and her lipstick went up to her nose in a bow and nearly half-way down her chin. Her skin had the brown look of leather. She and her ma, old Mary Meredith, lived in a lane off Rockford Avenue, and every evening you could see Tish standing with one hip jutting out at the foot of Marine Road, in the spills of rain, maybe. Her ma was never far away, but Tish stood on her own, looking towards the mailboat pier. If a man passed she would say 'Good evening' in the slow drawn-out voice the toffs used, and if he did not answer would step back out of his way and say 'Oh, pawr-don.' Once, Jack had gone with his da and ma to see Jimmy O'Dea in *Puss in Boots* in Dublin; it was pouring rain afterwards when they caught the last tram, and when it stopped at Dun Laoghaire he saw Tish and her mother climbing on like half-drowned rats.

On Sundays there was a queer shyness about her, as if that day was a private place she had no right to be in. Although she lived around the corner, she passed Jack and his da without a word or a look. Close up, there were moons of red chalk high on her cheeks and you could see her real lips, thin under the lipstick. When they were well past her his father said: 'Sure Tish is a harmless poor creature,' as if anyone had said to the contrary.

Further down the road, Mrs Threadgold was coming out of her house. Jack felt a twinge on seeing her. One day, years before, Johnny Quinn had brought him to her front door, knocked and then muttered something to Mrs Threadgold when she answered it. She had gone back into the house, and returned with two thick slices of bread and jam, one for each of them. Only then did Jack realize that Johnny had been begging. If his mother found out – she whose boast was that they paid their way, were under a compliment to no one and never wanted for anything, least of all nourishment – she would skin him; but worse than the fear was the shame. Mrs Threadgold had not looked at him in astonishment, but as if it was the most natural thing in the world to find him on her doorstep, seemingly begging for bread. He had hated her for it and for making him see himself, for that one instant, as no better than Johnny Quinn.

The chapel yard was jammed with people shoving out of one Mass and pushing in for the next. Mr Mundow, the decorator, was in charge of the money-plate at the two-penny door: you knew by the important stern look on his face that he was humble and proud of it, and he watched the pennies clattering down as if he were St Peter and they were Protestants going past him into Heaven. There were red ropes half-way down the aisles so that the two-pennies could not sneak into the sixpennies at the front. The quality and the Holy Marys sat near the altar, the cornerboys and wasters stood at the back where they would be first out, and the ordinary people sat between them. Jack tried to make room next to him for a woman with fat haunches and a terrible drooping eye that was an inch further down her face than the other one. He need not have troubled, for she made her own clearance by hitting him a sideways blow of her hips. Then she flopped to her knees, the cheeks of her behind flowing like tar over the flat of the bench, and began to pray. One eye was fixed on St Anthony and the other on Jack, and the rosary beads shot through her fingers at the rate you would haul in mackerel.

The benches filled, then the aisles. He was wondering how he would get through the crowd if he took weak when there was an appalling sound from behind him: a wheeze, a splutter and a hawking, all in one. He screwed his head around and saw Joe Healy with dribble on his chin and his face a blazing red. The redness was nothing new: there was a saying that you could read the racing results by Joe's face with the moon behind a cloud. He had chins that fell on one another like rolls of dough and a stomach that pulled his trousers open for three buttons down. Another saying was that he would drink Lough Erin dry, and he was stocious now, Sunday morning and all. He made another hawking noise, so terrible that the eyes of the man sitting next to him began to water; then his head sank and half-vanished into his chins.

The altar bell rang and Father Clarke came out. He was the nicest of the priests: he had been shell-shocked in the war and held his head cocked to one side. When you saluted him in the street he stopped for a shake-hands, and never asked if you had been a good boy or rubbish like that, but you moaned inside when he said the Mass, for it meant that Father Creedon would say the sermon.

Father Creedon was big and stout and his voice boomed like a fog-gun. When he climbed up the steps of the pulpit, sighing as if it was Mount Calvary, there were coughs and scufflings. Another priest would have begun to speak straight off and the noises would stop; but he waited. He stood stock-still, watching like a mouser until there was not even the creak of a bench, and then he waited again, as if for the whole town to fall quiet, house by house. The hush went on until you thought the chapel walls would fly asunder with the strain, and whatever caused the look of utter disgust on his face, you wanted to shout up and beg him not to blame you. Then, just as you were half-hoping that maybe he had dropped dead standing up, he let out a yell that would curdle milk. 'In the name of the Father, AND of the Son, AND of the HO-ly Ghost, AHHH-men!' There was such a thankful letting out of breath from the people that the candle flames shivered under the saints and Joe Healy muttered: 'Good man, yourself.'

The words dipped and rose again like hills, and Father Creedon coddled each one of them as a woman would nurse a child. Jack went off into a daydream. He was on this island, and a beautiful proud girl who was one of the quality had been shipwrecked with him. He knew the ending of the daydream, where she begged him to forgive her for having been so bad-mannered, but he could not work out how it would happen. It was a puzzler, and he was so busy racking his brains that he forgot one of the tricks Father Creedon used when he gave a sermon. He would let his voice drop to a whisper until he knew you were miles away and then give another of his roars. He did that today. His voice became hushed. 'And then,' he said, 'what did they do to Him? They led Him out of Jerusalem, they dragged Him up that hill of sorrow. And there ... THEY CRUCIFIED HIM!' People gave starts and little gasps, but Joe Healy put them all in the ha'penny place. He started out of his sleep, stood up and cried out: 'Jasus, where am I?'

Everyone gawked. His eyes were coming slowly open and there was a week's red stubble on his chin. When he saw the faces staring at him and realized where he was, he sat down again. That would have been the end of it, but Father Creedon went on looking at Joe the way you would look at a sweet, with the taste of it in your mind before you ate it. Then his voice shook the chapel. 'Will the man who is causing the disturbance please leave?'

Joe was already back asleep and making a sound like ten blue-bottles. There was another of Father Creedon's silences. His fat hands twitching on the rim of the pulpit put you in mind of fish dying on the harbour wall. 'I am referring,' he said, 'to the man sitting behind the boy with the fair hair. Will he *leave?*'

Jack cringed down in his seat at hearing himself pointed out for the whole chapel to look at. People were whispering to Joe and shaking him, and Father Creedon's face was like fire. 'Does that man want me to come down to him?' he boomed. 'I told him to get ... *out!*'

By now, the nudges and elbowings had wakened Joe. 'Is it the polis?' he asked, thinking he was back in the public house and the guards were in. He bent, groaning like a melodeon, to pick up his cap from the floor. Then he lost his balance. His boots hit the bench in front and he toppled out into the side aisle, slowly at first but ending with the crash of his bull head against the door of Father Creedon's own confession box.

At once there was a commotion as men crowded around him. People stood up to see. 'All you men are not necessary,' Father Creedon shouted from the pulpit, acting the gaffer. An angry muttering sound came from the cornerboys at the back of the chapel, and the priest whipped his head around and stared them silent the way you would stare down a growling dog. During all this, Father Clarke had been sitting in a chair like a throne at the side of the altar, but suddenly, with the sermon not half over, he was on his feet again and spouting prayers in Latin. He was hard of hearing, and some said afterwards that he had seen the people standing up to look at Joe and took it for a sign that Father Creedon had stopped preaching; but others said that it was not deafness but cuteness: that he had had enough of the blackguarding from the pulpit. Whichever it was, Father Creedon was left high and dry, with nothing for him to do but bless himself and go banging off into the vestry with his surplice swishing angrily. As for Joe, four men lifted him, his cap on his belly like a wreath on a coffin, and carted him out. When the Mass was over, Jack saw him again, lying on the grass in the priests' garden. His face had gone from red to the colour of turf-ash and two of the four men were bent over him. The people coming out of Mass gave sideways looks but did not stop, and as Jack turned to stare his da pulled him by the shoulder and said: 'Don't shame the man.'

There were two unpleasant things about Sundays: the first was Mass, the second was buying the newspapers at Mammy Reilly's. She was a little witch-faced woman, with dirt on her hands you could plant seed potatoes in. She wore boots, an old torn cardigan and a hair-net which held a clump of false hair the size of a bramble bush. Everyone knew that she kept her money inside her wig in sovereigns. It was Jack's job to buy the papers, for his da was afraid of her. One of her tricks with customers was to let on that she had come across a bill that was owing to her from the year dot. 'I've found this old account of yours,' she would say, grabbing at someone's sleeve with a hand that was like a bird's claw, 'and I'd like settlement, if you please.' Most people would pay the money for a quiet life, but Jack's da took to passing the shop on the far side of the street. 'Mr Keyes,' she would screech at him from her doorway, 'I want you!' He would walk faster and pretend not to hear, but his face was red with rage at being called out of his name.

Her shop was like none in the world. Once it had been like any other: Jack could remember when he was small, looking up at a high counter with a brass rail along the edge. But Mammy Reilly never sent back the newspapers she did not sell. By degrees they filled the shop, rising in towers to the ceiling itself, hiding the counter, crowding in so that there was no shop any more, only a tiny space inside the door where Mammy Reilly stood while her customers queued outside in the cold and rain. The window was filled with rusty toys, dummy cigarette packets and dead flies and wasps; nothing had been touched in years because it would take a mechanical digger to get near them. One of the great sights of Dalkey you could see any morning by squinting through the dirty glass of the front door. High up, where the newspapers nearly met the ceiling, you would see Mammy Reilly's head appear as she climbed a ladder at the far side. Then she squeezed through the space, swung her legs around and went sliding down into the shop, bumping up and down on the bales of paper as if her backside was a toboggan. In the evenings she would step out into the street, slam the door and lock it, first with a key and then by taking the door

72

knob with her, and get back to where she lived, behind the newspapers, by going through Da Lundy's sweet shop next door but one and over the back wall.

She never went to Mass, but nobody minded because she came from Belfast, so what else could you expect. One day her shop went on fire. She kept screaming and running back into it, and Father Creedon kept dragging her out again, telling her to resign herself to God's punishment for being a pagan. But the newspapers were wadded together so tightly that the fire went out of its own accord in disgust.

Today, when Jack's turn came to be served, she pushed the papers at him, then caught hold of him by the gansy. 'Tell your father I want him,' she said. As he got free of her and ran off, the hard prod of her finger still aching in his chest, he heard her lamenting to the rest of the queue that she was a poor wee good-natured creature who had fallen among robbers and Mohawks.

But now the day was clear and shining ahead. There would be red lemonade to drink with his dinner, the *Hotspur* to read afterwards, the great fuss of getting ready for the pictures and then the tram ride to Dun Laoghaire. His mother sat downstairs, his da and he on the top, and he was allowed to pay the fares ('Two three-ha'pennies and a penny, please') while the tram bucked and swayed, groaning down Bulloch hill and charging along the straight at Sandycove. In the Picture House his mother would peel an orange for the three of them and hand out caramels. The hullabaloo would deafen you, but it was nothing to the great screaming roar that went up when the curtains opened and on the screen you saw *Ace Drummond* (*Episode 12: Squadron of Death*). For years, Drummond the doorman had been persecuted by being called 'Bulldog' by the hard chaws in the fourpennies, and now, of course, they were calling him 'Ace'. The big picture today would be *Charlie Chan at the Opera*, which mightn't be too bad. His mother never guessed the murderer at a Charlie Chan: he always turned out to be someone she had taken a liking to, and she would let out a gasp and say: 'Oh, the Judas'; and when he was arrested or shot she would say: 'Well, that's the price of him.' After the pictures there would be tea, and at eight o'clock Chris and John would come to play Twenty-Fives for ha'pennies. 'My trick, I think, John,' Chris would say in a voice like pink icing on a cake, and John would answer: 'Just so, Chrissy.' His mother would grumble at her cards and say: 'Someone was hung in this seat,' and Chris's voice would go as high as an opera singer's: 'Oh, Mag, you're so comical.' When the visitors had gone home his da and ma would sit at opposite ends of the table studying tomorrow's runners, while he sat up in the big bed listening to the Sweepstakes programme on the wireless. 'Have you ever,' the soft voice would say, 'dreamed of a journey to the romantic islands of the South Seas?'

Running homewards with the papers under his oxter, he thought of the South Seas, then of his daydream at Mass, and then of Joe Healy unconscious in the priests' garden. He heard a bark and saw Jack the dog coming to meet him from the corner of the lane. Except for the dog and himself, Sorrento Road was empty, the houses winking back at him in the sun. He ran even faster, hurrying to open the bag of sweets that was Sunday.

Chapter 7

Two events marked my fourteenth year: I stopped going to confession and I killed Mrs Kelly who lived on our road.

My usual confessor was the shell-shocked Father Clarke, who had been a chaplain during the war. After four years in the trenches he regarded the sins committed in Dalkey as mere peccadilloes: which was why people entered and left his confessional with the rapidity of machine parts on an assembly line. Hardly had one door closed behind a penitent than the opposite one would bang open, revealing a Mass-misser or wife-beater dazed by his good fortune. For no one had ever managed to tell a sin to Father Clarke. You would kneel, the slide would fly back, a voice would whisper 'How long, my child?', and by the time you had told him he was already half-way through the absolution. Then, all in one breath, he would say: 'Three-Hail-Marys-pray-for-me-God-bless-you-my-child,' and the slide was rammed shut again. A friend of mine had somehow managed to put his hand on a girl's knee and was thereafter so consumed by remorse and pride in equal quantities that he became determined to tell all to Father Clarke. Such a dreadful and splendid sin could not, he believed, be absolved in the usual conveyor-belt manner: it must be properly confessed and chastised. The moment the slide was pulled back, he was off like a sprinter. 'I done a terrible thing, Father,' he whispered. 'And, God bless you, you're sorry,' the priest said and at once launched into the absolution. 'Father, Father, will you wait!' my friend hissed, getting panicky, and stuck a finger through the wire mesh to keep the slide from closing. The only result was that he nearly lost the finger.

So I was not unduly alarmed when my mother one day decided that it was high time I went to confession. Such was Father Clarke's popularity that the pews outside his confessional were usually crowded with penitents shuffling sideways on their knees and almost falling over in their efforts to match his unflagging speed,

75

while only a few people waited outside Father Creedon's box across the church. But today a handwritten card pinned to the green curtains announced that Father Clarke had been promoted to a parish of his own in Kildare. My sense of personal loss was quickly overtaken by the realization that I must make my confession to Father Creedon.

We were all mortally afraid of Credo, as we called him behind his back. He moved and spoke majestically, never referring to himself simply as a priest, but as 'a priest of God', rather as if his ordination had been in the nature of a personal appointment by Divine warrant. Neither, for example, could he refer merely to the family rosary and let it go at that: it was invariably 'that grand and glorious old Irish custom'. He was the terror of the altar boys and choirboys. Two years previously, I had been coerced into joining the choir and, being an incurable croaker then, as I still am, I spent the next six months merely opening and closing my mouth, but taking care not to let a sound emerge. One day at Benediction I became carried away and actually joined in the *Tantum Ergo*. The altar was at the far end of the church from the choir loft, but I saw Credo's bull head swivel around and fix us with a blood-curdling look of outrage that silenced not only me but half the choir as well. On his way back into the sacristy he paused to bellow above the words of the closing hymn: 'The choir will not leave the church,' and I knew the jig was up. It took him five minutes to disrobe and confront us, and another five to identify and expel the crow.

If Father Clarke shot through confessions at the speed of light, Credo made a meal of each one. No one, not even a daily communicant, escaped in less than five minutes, and some were with him for fifteen. We waited, listening to the rumble of his voice that was like a bus crossing a metal bridge. Once, we distinctly heard him say 'Oh, my God' in seeming horror and we glued our eyes to the door, agog to see what kind of depraved creature would emerge. A shudder ran through the penitents when it proved to be a girl who could not have been older than nine.

At last my turn came. I entered the box, knelt and waited. Great martyred sighs were coming from beyond the wall, and I heard him say: 'How many times?' and 'Did you wallow in it?' Bored, I rested my chin on the edge of the tiny wooden shelf in front of me, rolled my eyes up and pretended to be the decapitated John the Baptist.

There was a mumble of Latin, the sound of a slide closing, a grunt as Credo shifted on his chair, and then a large blue eye was regarding me through the cruciform aperture in the wire mesh. That in itself was unusual: all one ever saw of Father Clarke was his ear. I stared in fascination at the unblinking eye.

'Begin,' a voice groaned.

I started to gabble. 'Bless me, Father, for I have sinned. It was two months, Father, since my last conf –'

'Stop!' The naked ferocity would have halted a rabid dog in its tracks.

'What age are you?'

'Thirteen, Father.'

'And in all those thirteen years has no one ever instructed you as to the proper manner of receiving the sacrament of Penance?'

I tried to think of what atrocity I could have possibly committed. Was there, I wondered, a private peephole through which he had witnessed my impersonation of John the Baptist? He waited; then the eye moved away and, familiarly, I saw an ear. Father Clarke had hairs sprouting from his; Credo's was pink and small.

'You will say the *Confiteor*.'

So that was it. Most priests, even those who would have regarded Father Clarke as a speed fiend, allowed you to say the *Confiteor* privately before you entered the box. It saved time. But Credo was a reactionary: he favoured one-hour Masses and half-hour sermons; Lionel Barrymore could not have sucked more juice from a death scene than Credo did from saying one Hail Mary.

I began the *Confiteor*. 'I confess to Almighty God, to Blessed Mary ever Virgin, to Blessed Michael the Archangel, to Blessed John the Baptist, to . . .' And there I stuck.

'Begin again,' Credo said.

This time, so paralysed was my brain from fear, I got no further than Michael the Archangel. Credo's eye had returned to glare at me again, and I could no more have remembered the *Confiteor* than a Muslim could have recited a passage from the Talmud. Fatally, I began to mumble gibberish in the hope that he would assume I had become incoherent from sheer religious fervour.

'Get out of this box!'

It was a roar so loud that it must have been audible in Castle Street.

'You will kneel before the high altar and pray. When the Confessions are over I will give you a prayer book and you will learn that grand and glorious prayer, the *Confiteor*. Now get out.'

As I left the box, twenty pairs of eyes followed me from the pews, perhaps in pity, certainly in stupefaction that one thin, grubby boy could have sinned so execrably. I started down the aisle, faint with shame. My life in those days seemed to be a succession of disasters – I was the kind of youngster who, if he sneaks up a dark laneway to pee, discovers that he is doing it on the boot of a lurking policeman – but this was the worst yet. In our family, not even my uncle Sonny had ever been put out of a confession box.

The thought of having to face Credo again after the Confessions was too much to bear. Instead of kneeling before the altar, I fled out by the sanctuary door, walked a mile to Glasthule and had my confession heard by an elderly priest who told me that impure thoughts would turn me into a degenerate. Shattering as the incident with Credo had been, I thought I had heard the last of it. But that afternoon my father came home from work grinning with fury.

'A nice thing,' he said as my mother stared from him to me, 'a nice thing when the priest gets down off of his shaggin' bicycle to stop me on the public road.'

I could hardly believe my ears, but it was true. Father Creedon had blabbed the whole story. The boy, he said, had defied a directive from of a priest of God. And that was not all. When, Credo wanted to know, had we last knelt down as a family to recite that grand and glorious prayer, the *Confiteor*? Whereupon, carried away, he began to boom out the words in the middle of Station Road, smiting himself mightily in the chest when he got to '. . . through my fault, through my fault, through my most grievous fault,' with my father in his working boots, collarless shirt and battered hat gaping at him and aware that men were coming out of the bookie's to watch the performance. What most annoyed my father was not my theological shortcomings, but that he had regarded the clergy with coolness ever since they had excommunicated the diehards during the Civil War and now I had given Credo the chance to lord it over him. 'There he was,' my father said, 'roaring the I Confess at me in front of the town and bating the shite out of himself with his fist.'

78

My mother, of course, looked at me as if I had suddenly grown a forked tail. 'Well, it's the price of me,' she said, 'for rearing a heathen.'

I could not have cared less about either of them. I had been betrayed. Only the previous week I had seen a picture called *Thou Shalt Not Kill* at the Astoria, with Charles Bickford as a priest who was ready to let an innocent man go to the electric chair sooner than repeat what he had heard in the confessional. And Father Creedon had told, even without being asked. He had not exactly revealed a sin, of course, but I was in no humour to split hairs. There is nothing sweeter than righteousness, especially when it provides an excuse for escaping from what was a bore in the first place; and henceforth I was done with confession. It was a private resolve – my principles did not quite extend to informing my parents – and I became expert at sidling out of the church under cover of the horde of communicants jostling towards the altar. For giving up confession meant, of course, avoiding communion as well. The prospect of spending the rest of one's life in a state of unshriven sin was uncomfortable enough; committing sacrilege on top of it was plainly asking for trouble. If ever I stood in need of a friendly priest, however, it was after the killing of old Mrs Kelly a few months later.

Mrs Kelly lived with her middle-aged daughter, Josie, in a cottage on our road. She was plagued by 'bad turns', and on these occasions would lie in bed in the front room praying feebly, the rosary beads entwined in her fingers. Her life's journey was done; she was at the point of arrival at the shadowy terminus where, just beyond the buffers, the angels were waiting to meet her train and waft her onwards. Inevitably, however, the engine driver would change his mind at what seemed the last minute, and the locomotive would chug into reverse, bearing Mrs Kelly back several stations down the line. Whenever she fell ill, my mother was sent for and, to labour the metaphor, took charge of the dining car, plying the invalid with beef tea and fingers of toast. It was her function, too, to sigh 'God's holy will be done' whenever the old lady whimpered: 'I'm going this time, Mrs Keyes, I've lit me last holy candle,' for among their class and age there was a rigid protocol to be observed at times of sickness. When a person was really dying, you were jollity itself, wheezing with laughter and swearing to them by every holy picture in the room

79

that by tomorrow they would be hopping about like a two-year-old. The opposite applied if all that ailed them was an attack of wind or a gall-stone. Then you sighed and were Job's comforter. 'Didn't you get to a good age?' you said, and reminded them to say a prayer for you on their discharge from Purgatory. And the poor creature would murmur that she was already within hailing distance of her beloved Mick or Paddy, who had gone before, and you agreed with her, banishing from your mind the reflection that Mick or Paddy used to beat her good-looking every night of their married life and was, if there was any justice, well charred by now in the other place. My mother's own sick-bed experiences tending to my grandmother made her an expert at the fine art of extracting every drop of lugubrious pleasure from a neighbour's illness.

In November of that year Mrs Kelly fell ill again and my mother set off with a mug of beef tea and our wire toasting fork. My own plans for the evening consisted of a visit to the Carnegie Library in Dun Laoghaire and an hour or so of colloguing with a crony of mine on the Barrack Road. My friend's mother had won five-hundred pounds in a crossword competition and had not been quite right in the head every since. She believed herself to be surrounded by predators intent on robbing her and had even banished her husband to permanent exile in a back room on the theory that propinquity bred cupidity. Her moods were such that I never knew whether I would have the front door slammed in my face with a sharp 'There's nothing for you here' or be welcomed and given cocoa. This, however, proved to be one of the cocoa evenings, and by the time my friend and I had argued the relative merits of firing a six-gun from the hip or taking proper aim and fanning the hammer, it was nearly eleven o'clock.

Hurrying along Sorrento Road, I saw a light on behind the drawn blind in Mrs Kelly's front window and realized that my mother was still there. The idea occurred to me to let her know that I was safely on my way home, so I took a penny from my pocket and rapped sharply on the glass. For a moment there was silence. Then a voice which was not my mother's cried out in piercing terror: 'The Dead Man's Knock! The Dead Man's Knock!'

If there was alarm within the house, there was paralysis outside it. I stood frozen: partly with shock, partly with dismay that I had yet again come to grief. It seemed only sensible to call out 'It's only me,' but before I could do so Mrs Kelly started to whinny and wail, beseeching my mother to save her. I fled.

My father, who became peevish whenever my mother was obliged to be out late, had gone to bed. He called out from the back room: 'Is that you, Mag?'

'It's me.'

'In the name of Jasus, what hour of the night is this to be coming in at?' Then, without waiting for an answer: 'Will you get to bed before she comes in on the top of you and there's blood spilt.'

'Yes, da.'

The back room of our house was the kitchen; it held a dresser, a table, wooden chairs, a gas stove and a double bed where my parents slept. The front room was always referred to with fitting deference as 'the room' and contained a black wardrobe, a sideboard, two balding furry armchairs and a matching divan which was my bed. It held our treasures: two coloured photographs of Blackpool, God knows how come by, china dogs, fancy egg cups that had once held Easter eggs, brass fire irons, the good – the only – tea service and a silver flower holder containing honesty. Apart from serving as my bedroom, it was used only at Christmas and on the solemnest of social occasions. In our town, as elsewhere, even the smallest cottage was and still is divided in two: one part for living in, the other as an ideal, a regret and an aspiration, all in one.

I closed the door between 'the room' and the kitchen and switched on the light. Mrs Kelly's screams were still in my head like a marble in a kettle, but at least there was no one who could identify me as the cause of them. After a while I began to snigger, thinking how best to embellish the story at school. Then, sitting on the edge of the bed, I opened one of my library books. It was *Dracula*. Two hours later, I was still reading and shaking with fright, but even more afraid to turn off the light and go to bed lest I saw a ray of moonlight – which was one of the Count's methods of entering a room – or heard the flutter of bat's wings against the ceiling. By the time my mother came in my blood had chilled to a degree sufficient to repel any discriminatory vampire. I heard her footsteps in the lane and made a rush for the light switch, but she was already in the room.

When I received no tongue-lashing at being found still up and with the light on at one a.m., I knew something was drastically wrong. She put her hat in the wardrobe, sighing gently to herself, but with a suppressed air of great excitement. I still wonder what kept me from fainting when she said at last:

'Me poor old neighbour is gone. But we knew there was no hope for her from the minute we heard the Dead Man's Knock.'

My next clear memory is of lying in bed the following evening. Over the head of the bed there hung a large oleograph of Christ wearing the crown of thorns, his eyes turned upwards in agony. Flat on my back, I saw the face upside down so that now he was squinting downwards at me, and I had never seen such malevolent eyes. The realization that I had killed Mrs Kelly came back in dizzying waves. I remembered a sentence from *Dracula* – 'For the dead travel fast' and fully expected to see her appear at the foot of the bed, dressed in the brown habit in which she was at that moment being waked.

I began to have nightmares. Once, I woke up babbling in delirium, and my mother gave me a Seidlitz powder and sprinkled me with Lourdes water while I drank it. At school I was catatonic. I had always been an insufferable know-it-all, forever raising my hand and chanting 'Sir, sir!' to volunteer such jewels of information as that the harp was the most difficult instrument to play, and there was widespread glee when the headmaster – known as 'Tabac' (the Irish for 'tobacco') – slammed me across the ears daily for inattention. Five minutes with a friendly priest would have dispelled my terrors. What kept me from confession, however, was not my principles (I was no longer in a condition to have any), but a mental vision of Father Creedon alighting from his bicycle on Station Road to delight my father with the tidbit that his son had broken the grand and glorious old fifth commandment and was now a juvenile Crippen.

In time, my feelings of guilt faded, leaving in their place a conviction that I was one of nature's outcasts. The idea occurred to me that, having committed the worst sin in the calendar, I was destined to break the other nine commandments as well. Call it a temporary derangement, but the thought became an obsession; it grew inside my head like a baby cuckoo in a strange nest; it told me that I was fated in time to desecrate a church, commit perjury, rob a bank, and worse. My future was a wasteland of iniquity.

I cannot now remember clearly how I decided to break all the remaining commandments at once and have done with it. Perhaps it occurred to me that if I gave the devil his due he might leave me in peace, or I may have chosen to commit the sins now in a modest way rather than suffer the inconveniences of jail and the hangman later on. At any rate, once the decision was made my heart became lighter; already I felt purged.

I began in fine style. The first commandment – 'I am the Lord, thy God; thou shalt not have strange Gods before Me' – was child's play: I simply sneaked into the Methodist church on Rockfort Avenue, genuflected before the communion table and shot out again, my knees trembling from the sheer unholiness of the place. 'Thou shalt honour thy father and thy mother' was even easier: I made hideous faces at them when their backs were turned. And with consummate cunning I broke both the seventh and eighth commandments in one manoeuvre: I stole Peadar O'Loughlin's pencil at school and then bore false witness by telling him that 'Bomber' Young was the thief. This was strategy of a high order. 'Bomber', who was nicknamed after Joe Louis, had the physique, bearing and temperament of a pigmy gorilla, and I knew that Peadar, whose limbs were like matchsticks, would use his own blood for ink sooner than go looking for his pencil within range of those bone-mangling hands.

Five to go. It was the work of an instant to take the name of the Lord my God in vain. Profaning the Sabbath day was more difficult, but I solved it (and settled an old score) by positioning myself at the church gates and scandalizing the Mass-goers with a brazen imitation of Father Creedon at his most orotund. Pushing my belly out to suggest a paunch, I droned: 'Yass, yass, what a grand and glorious old Irish morning it is, to be sure, and today there will be a grand and glorious special collection!' An elderly woman terminated the performance by flailing at me with her prayer book and hissing 'Well, you bloody little jeer,' but the deed was done.

It took no prodigious effort of will to covet my neighbour's goods, but coveting his wife seemed a more futile exercise, especially since my neighbours were Tim and Essie Quirk, both white-haired and in their seventies. Nonetheless, I can still remember streeling into their back room on some pretext, sitting at the kitchen table and coveting Mrs Quirk so passionately that my eyes crossed. 'That child,' she remarked to her husband, 'needs his roof thatched.'

The remaining sin, adultery, caused me more trouble than the rest of them strung together. To begin with, I had no idea of what it involved, and my first attempt to find out caused me to run foul of Father Creedon yet again. Once a week we had religious instruction at school and it was always given by one of the priests, with Tabac standing by, his jaws working furiously whenever there was a wrong answer. It was said that he had been shot in the stomach during the Civil War. He belched and broke wind continuously and had recourse to a jar of white powder on his desk. It was, I think, Morty Mooney who topped up the jar one day with Glauber salts, which later precipitated a pogrom unseen since Cromwell's visit to Drogheda. Tabac's temper was ungovernable; if a boy misbehaved during the catechism class he waited until the priest had gone, then went wild. His face turned to a murky purple, he grabbed a cane from under his desk and began slashing with it, first at the air, then at the hands of the offender, catching the backs of the fingers with each upstroke and quite literally farting with fury.

Today, our catechist was Father Creedon. He boomed out questions for some minutes, then gave us one of his homilies. The theme was the dangers of bad company and he ended by imploring any boy in need of spiritual advice to go straight to a 'priest of God'. Like a fool, I on the instant raised my hand and began snapping my fingers. Tabac's bald head shot around, and I saw Credo's face become puckered like a perished balloon as he recognized me.

'Yass?'

'Please, Father, what's adultery?'

There was a silence, then a convulsive fart. Credo seemed not to hear it. Without looking at Tabac, he asked: 'Is this an example of the filth that goes on in your classroom, Mr Mullen?'

In my innocence, I thought he was referring to the fart. Then, before the boys could rise, as we did whenever a visitor entered or departed, he was gone, slamming the door after him, and before we could sit down again Tabac was dragging me across the floor by the hair of the head. 'You miserable bowsy, you'd shame us, would you?' he raged, fumbling for the cane. Luckily for me, his anger was such that it ruined his aim, and I ended up more frightened than damaged. The mystery concerning adultery deepened, particularly as I became known as an incorrigible wag and had only to mention the word in the schoolyard to evoke howls of mirth. Probably no one else knew, either.

The last person I would normally ask for information or advice was my father. But on the Saturday evening I suddenly blurted out: 'Da, I have to commit adultery and I don't know how.'

He was soaking his feet in a tin bath of warm water, the preliminary to paring his corns. My mother was at my grandmother's. He said: 'You have to do what?'

'Commit adultery, Da.'

He seemed more mystified than shocked. 'And what do you want to do a stunt the like of that for?'

'I have to.'

Naturally I could not confide in him about Mrs Kelly or the subsequent mental algebra that had led to my present straits. His face was so blank that I began to wonder if even he knew what adultery was.

'Say it to me again.'

'Adultery, Da.'

He repeated the word, then said: 'Whisht, now, till I dry my feet.' I waited. His feet were neat and white, the toes straight. Once, he gave a chuckle and said: 'Oh, a comical boy.'

When he had finished buffing his insteps with the towel he told me to empty the tin bath down the shore in the yard and fill a jug with water from the tap. I did as I was bid. He was waiting for me with a cup in one hand and a milk jug in the other. 'Adultery,' he said again, and I nodded.

I watched, mesmerized, as he solemnly poured milk into the cup until it was half full. Then he took the jug that contained water and filled the cup to the brim. He thrust it under my nose.

'There,' he said triumphantly, 'that's adultery!'

He was, I know now, in dead earnest. But at the time, and although I could not understand what all the fuss had been about, his word was good enough for me.

Chapter 8

He was nearly fourteen, but still his da insisted on going with him to the school on his first day.

When word came that he had won the scholarship his mother did the rounds of every huxter's shop in the town from Winnie Carthy's to Annie Toole's, asking to know which school she should send him to: the Christian Brothers' in Dun Laoghaire or Presentation College in Glasthule. In reality she no more wanted advice than a cat wanted the mange: it was her way of spreading the news, of rubbing the town's nose in it that the Keyeses were on the rise at long last.

The first person she told was Mrs Costello who lived at the top of the lane and kept hens. There were more Costellos than you could count; they fought all day like ginger toms, but look crossways at any one of them and it was not a family that faced you but an army. Mrs Costello was taller than his da and had red hair. 'Everyone to their own taste,' she said, giving Jack a look as if he was one of her hens. 'The national schools are good enough for *my* childer and sorra one of them the worst for it.'

'Sure the whole nine of them is a credit to you,' Jack's mother said in a voice that threatened desolation to anyone who dared say to the contrary, and as soon as Jack and herself were clear of the Costellos' gate she elbowed him with delight and said: 'The old rip is ragin'.'

She was so full of herself with the news that she even told uncle Sonny, forgetting in her excitement that she had been black out with him since Jack's grandmother had died the previous January. Mary had come to live in Kalafat Lane, sharing the big bed with his mother, while he and his da slept head to toe on the sofa; and although Sonny was glad to see the last of her and could now get married to Kate Fortune from the Dargle Laundry, he complained to the town that his poor afflicted sister had been stolen from under his roof. He was a great man for having his cake and eating it. He even sent a letter written in pencil to Jack's mother saying: 'Yous have take Mary off me yous are reponbil for her now you can kep and cloth her I have nutting to do.' The letter was not signed, for it was a belief of Sonny's that he could keep in the clear with the law by never putting his name to anything.

When he heard about the scholarship his eyes were as unwinking as two black currants. He gave a smile that was higher at one side than the other and said: 'You'll be a good fella to borry money from some day.'

'Oh, Jack's the boy with the brains,' Jack's da said with a laugh that had a sob in it.

'Aye, but there's brains *and* brains,' Sonny answered, as if to say that it was not cleverness that had won the scholarship, but a kind of go-by-the-wall cuteness.

Jack's da was too slow to take Sonny's meaning, but in an instant the Doyle look was on his mother's face and she turned on him like a whippet after a hare, her voice like sticks breaking. 'It's no wonder you never had a minute's luck,' she said to him. 'And signs on it, neither will you. You were always a begrudger and you wouldn't give a body ditch.'

With that, she left Sonny standing by his half-door, the twisted smile still glued to his face, and pushed Jack ahead of her down the path, with his da trotting to catch up and saying: 'Sure, Mag, the man never opened his mouth.'

Like all the Doyles, she had a skin like tissue paper, and they could no more pull together than if they were at opposite ends of a tug-o'-war. But it was with aunt Chris that the worst falling out happened, the time his mother visited her in hospital. Chris lived on Burdett Avenue in Sandycove in a house with stairs in it and coloured glass around the hall door and was always careful to keep her and John's friends to one side of her and people like Sonny and Mary and Jack's parents to the other. It was as if she lived on top of a wall that was built too high to be seen across. On Sundays, she and John would call after tea to Kalafat Lane, where she would hold her cards at Twenty-Fives as if her fingers were sugar tongs. Jack could see his mother looking at Chris's ring with the diamond in it as if it was a rat that needed braining. Her voice would put you in mind of Tish Meredith saluting a sailor off the mailboat. 'Mai trick, Ai think,' she would say with a squeak of a laugh, and his mother would rush into the scullery to scald the teapot and mutter: 'You'd think she had a poker stuck up her.'

One day Chris was in St Michael's Hospital with something that ailed her, and his mother paid her a visit. While they were talking, a well-dressed woman came into the ward and Chris's face turned from everyday pink to red. The woman handed her a bag of grapes and looked curiously at his mother, who was there in her black stockings, the hat she had worn since old God's time and the bit of baldy fur with the one-eyed fox's head she wore around her collar. Jack did not have to be there to see her primping herself and waiting to be introduced: she loved mixing with well-off people and proving she was a match for the best of them.

'This,' said Chris from the bed, 'is my friend Mrs Mornahan. And this is Mrs Keyes.'

Not a word about her being Chris's sister. She could not credit it. She waited, thinking it had slipped Chris's mind, but no: the pair of them were deep in talk, and not a sign was given that she was there at all. She got up and went out, her knees shaking under her from rage and weakness, and a month later when the Bennetts came calling she turned them from the door.

That quarrel was in the past, and Chris clapped her hands with delight when she heard of the scholarship. Polite little bells rang in her voice, and uncle John tried to get a word in edgeways, like a plumber mending a leak. 'That's excellent news,' he said, bending so that two Jacks appeared in his glasses. 'Oh, full marks. Just so.'

Chris's smile would sweeten a lemon. 'It's the chance of a lifetime, Mag,' she sang. 'He'll end up in the civil service yet, like his uncle John.'

'Please God,' his mother sighed. 'For them that lives to see it.' It was amazing how much meaning she could cram into a sentence. Her life's work was done, she was telling them; the sacrifices had been made, and now there was nothing left for her to do but die from the strain of it.

'But, Mag,' Chris said, not minding her ulagoning, 'don't send him to the Christian Brothers. Such a common crowd goes there, every rag, tag and bobtail off the Bus Lawn, letting on to be gentlemen. Catch *them* being let into the civil service!' At the thought of such an impossibility she gave a laugh like spoons falling. 'No, Mag, send him to the Presentation. That's where the O'Shaughnessy boys go.'

His heart jumped. Presentation College was what he longed for: not just to be friends with the fair-haired O'Shaughnessys, whom he knew to nod to and who nodded back, but because in his mind Presentation was like Greyfriars School in *The Magnet*. He read *The Magnet* every week from front to back, and the people in it, like Billy Bunter, the Famous Five of the Remove, Croker the bully, Skinner the sneak and Mr Quelch the acidulous form master, were more real to him than Tommy Kinsella who lived opposite. It was a place where the quality went, and in such a different world you could not but be a different person. On his birth certificate his name was John Byrne, but in Dalkey he was called Jack Keyes. His real self was somewhere between the two names, for he had no wish to be the first and no right to be the second. But at the new school he would begin at last to be that third in-between person who was neither.

His mother was forever saying that to look at Chris you would think she had never gone barefoot in her puff, but it was seldom she went against her advice. So Presentation was decided upon. She took him down to the school during the summer holidays, and there they met the Superior, Brother Berchmans Morley. Jack saw eyes like the sea in March, a small thin mouth and a long nose – he would learn in time that the boys' nickname for him was 'Schnozzle'. His black robes hissed like snakes as he walked and gave out the smell of ironing. He cut his words short as if with a nail scissors, so that they came out as 'Em plissed to mit you, Mrs Kizz.' He gave Jack a long look from floor to thatch through glasses that were gold-framed like uncle John's and took his mother into a room for what he called 'a privvit word'. Jack sat on a chair of polished bog oak that was too high for him, letting his feet swing until his boot heels hit the underside of it. There was a scent of wax and carbolic mixed, and he heard distant kitchen noises. A tall painted statue of Our Lord stood on a shelf above a door, with the wounded hands spread out as if to say: 'Are you sure you're comfortable?' He banged his fists on his knees with the excitement of being in Presentation. He saw himself a month from now saying words out of *The Magnet* like 'beastly' and 'top-hole' and running across the Quad – of course in places like Harold Boys' School in Dalkey they just called it 'the yard' – to shout 'I say, you chaps!' Jasus, it would be great.

After a few minutes, his mother came out of the room. Brother Berchmans held open the heavy front door for them and said: 'Ah'll see that the boy gets mah special attention, Mrs Kizz.' The air outside had a sharpness that caught at his throat after the smell of wax.

At the tram stop his mother had a moony look on her face. 'He told me I was a great woman,' she said, nearly crooning it.

He had no need to ask why. He knew that she had been spouting out of her to Brother Berchmans about how she had adopted him when his own didn't want him and how she had reared him through thick and thin and feast and famine. She could no more keep it to herself than she could stop from blessing herself when passing a chapel; it was her way of showing off what a great woman she was. He felt his insides go empty at the thought that Brother Berchmans might let out his secret for the whole school to know; then he thought of the masters at Greyfriars and how they were stern but fair, and he felt easier in his mind.

He had been to two schools: Loreto Convent when he was small, and Harold Boys'. All he could remember from the convent was the day his pen slipped and rolled down his copybook leaving laneways of black ink from top to bottom. There was no way of hiding it, for Sister Ita walked between the desks with her head turning like an egg whisk. When she saw the copybook her hands shot out from under her habit and she gave a cry of disgust. 'What's this? What's this?' she shouted. She had grey eyes, and her face was a nun's face, red from scrubbing. He began to stutter, but she picked up the copybook and tore out the page. She pulled him to his feet and pinned the page to the back of his gansy. 'Dirty child,' she said into his face.

He wore the page on his back all day. At playtime he tried to hide it by standing against a wall, but Sister Ita dragged him into the middle of the play-yard. 'Stay there,' she said, 'for the world to know the price of you.' He stayed whingeing where he was put, and it came into his head that the more he wanted to be like the Chap in the serial at the Picture House, the more people kept treating him like the Bully instead. The matter of the spilled ink and the page pinned to his back would have been forgotten and done with if Teasie Costello had not come knocking at the house that evening with the big mouth on her. When his mother answered the door she said all in one breath: 'Mrs Keyes, Mammy said to tell you that Jack got ink all over his good copybook and Sister Ita pinned the page to his back and he had to wear it all day and-and-and Miss O'Kelly cem outa the Senior Infants and saw him and gev him a push and said "Go 'long, you messer." '

Next day, his da went with him to the school and sent him in to tell Sister Ita that she was wanted. To make it worse, she was in one of her good humours, and it would have been a cushy day with her. 'Your daddy wants to see me?' she said. 'What antrumartins have you been up to?' She gave him a pat on the head as if the pair of them were the best of butties and sailed out into the hall. At once the classroom was filled with noise and chattering; then the talking died down, bit by bit, as his da's voice came through the folding partition. He was shouting. 'I had a sister of me own,' he said, 'that's dead and gone – Sister Mary Gonzales that was in the Blind Asylum at Merrion Gates beyant – and she never done to a child the like of what you done.' There was more, until he began to splutter and hem and haw with the rage he was in, and at last the front door slammed and the partition shook and Sister Ita came back into the room. Her face was the colour of the band of white cloth across her forehead. 'Jack Keyes,' she said, 'kneel out here.'

When at first he did not move her voice went high and dangerous. 'Out, out!' He stood before her. She took him by the shoulders, spinning him around to face the class, and pushed him to his knees. She slapped her hands together once, then buried them in her sleeves. If she had had slanty eyes she could have passed for Charlie Chan. She was panting. 'Say after me,' she said, ' "I swear by all the blessed saints ... that I will never again ... carry tales out of this school ... or may I answer for it on the day of Final Judgement." '

He said the words. It would have been no use to tell her that the tale carrier was not him but Teasie Costello. Once they had it in their minds that you were the Bully, it was a waste of time trying to act the Chap.

His second school was Harold Boys' on the Bus Lawn. It was built of red brick, and for the first two years your master was Alfie O'Hagan, who was an old fellow of maybe fifty, with a calm, wide face. He moved slowly. When you got an answer right, he shook your hand and tightened his grip until the bones bent and you came twisting up from your desk and under his arm like a tango dancer. If you refused his hand, he was offended. 'Are you making strange with me?' he would ask, his eyes dreaming at the ceiling while he twisted the lobe of your ear like an orange peel, and 'No, sir!' you screamed. Squeezing hands and ears was a sign that he liked you; with the dodgers and mitchers he used the cane and his fists.

After Alfie, you went to Tabac, the headmaster. He was bald, and whenever the pain in his stomach gave him lackery he would grind his jaws half out of their sockets, and woe betide you. Away to one side of the play-yard there were rows of flowerbeds the size of the graves in Dean's Grange, and it was Tabac's idea that every boy in sixth class would have his own bed for a year to grow flowers in. It was holy murder. You could kneel and trowel until your back broke, and at the end of it the sight of one weed was enough to send Tabac into a dribbling, dancing fit.

When Jack was given a flowerbed of his own he asked his da for seeds: the kind, he said, that would fend for themselves without minding or coaxing and, above all, would bloom so thickly as to hide the weeds in between. Explaining a thing to his da was like driving a nail into a brick; just when you thought he understood he would start romancing about Amy Robsarts or delphiniums or chrysanths. But long suffering comes at last, and one evening he came home from Jacobs' with a packet of seeds. 'Don't go mad now,' he said. 'A few of these will do you.'

It seemed silly not to use them all. It stood to reason that the more seeds you sowed, the more flowers you would have. Next day, Jack started to empty the packet over his plot. ('Don't plant them,' his da had said. 'Sprinkle the buggers.') As the first seeds came out of the packet a gust of wind whisked them across the play-yard, so he waited until it was calm, then knelt and carefully emptied out what was left. He prayed there would be enough.

The following week the pains in Tabac's stomach were so bad that he was ordered to his bed in the house next door to the school. While he was still laid up, Jack thought he noticed a pink flush the length of his flowerbed. At first it was like something seen out of the corner of the eye: the harder you looked, the faster it vanished. Next day, there was no mistake: the flowers were growing; and by the time the week was out the flowerbed looked like a great funeral wreath. They were the only ugly flowers he had ever seen: they would put you in mind of the pink foam in a cough bottle after it was shaken. Every day there were more of them. What was worse, they began to spread to the other allotments. Morty Mooney, who had planted primulas, nearly dropped out of his standing to see the wrong kind of flowers coming up. Fatboy Brennan said it was Jack's fault and threatened to be dug out of him while Peadar O'Loughlin, who talked Irish to his sisters and was Tabac's pet, spent all of the play hour on his knees crying and trying to pull up the pink flowers by their roots without disturbing the hyacinths his old fellow had bought for him from Watson's nurseries. But the threats and the moans stopped the day the gravel of the play-yard itself began to turn pink. The whole school just stood and looked at it. There was nothing anyone could think of to say, except for Bomber Young, who was a born curser and who said: 'Oh, Jasus'.

Jack grew weak thinking of what Tabac would do to him. The waiting was the worst part, and one night in bed he made up his mind to go to him at home and get it over with there and then, instead of in front of the whole school. It was too late, for the following morning Tabac decided he was feeling better and got out of bed. When he looked through the window and saw that the school yard had turned into what looked like a pink meadow that needed scything it was nearly the end of him. He let out a screech louder than when the Free Stater shot him in the stomach in 1922, but it was nothing to the noises that came out of his other end.

Before the day was out a man was spraying weed-killer the length and breadth of the yard. It was the end, too, of the allotments for that year, for the beds were dug up as Tabac looked on, grey in the face and with his teeth grinding like mincers as if he was trying to save his strength and use it up, both at once. Jack waited to be informed on by one of the school Judases, but nothing was said. He thought at first it was because they were thankful to him for putting an end to the gardening; but Mocky Duggan told him: 'We didn't want your corpse on our consciences.' In fact, the only mention of the pink flowers was when Father Creedon came in one day to teach catechism. He blessed himself like a workman heaving bricks and started off. It was a parable: 'The sower went out to sow his seed, and as he sowed some fell by the wayside . . .' Tabac was standing between the desks. He bent down and hissed into Jack's ear: 'And by Jasus, Keyes, he had nothing on you!'

One evening, Jack asked his da what the pink flowers were called. 'Oh, begod, them's from the country of Japan,' his da said. 'What is it now they call them?' He thought about it until it came to him. 'Oh, aye . . . Mother o' Millions.'

It was his mother's idea for his da to go with him on his first day at Presentation. When he asked to be let take the tram on his own she looked at him as if reading his mind. ' 'Deed and you will not,' she said. 'People'd think you had no one belonging to you!' So they went off together: he in his new purple blazer, his da wearing his black winter top coat over his working clothes. At Gilbey's corner he looked sideways at the old hat rammed square on his da's head, at the caked clay on his half-mast trousers, at his boots bent like the rockers of a cradle. He thought of the pair of them walking into Presentation.

'Da, you go on up to Jacobs'. I'll get the tram and we'll tell her you came with me.'

'Not at all, son,' his da said gaily. 'I won't desert you, never fear.'

Flann Hartigen was on the tram. Jack knew him to see; he was a Presentation boy. The way he walked, like someone trying not to step in dung, had given him the nickname of 'the Cow' Hartigen. He was sixteen but still wore short trousers. People in Dalkey said that he was half-touched. He had a drawled-out don't-cha-know accent like Lord Mauleverer in *The Magnet* and had been put out of the Carnegie Library for pushing an invisible wheelbarrow in front of him and asking people to move out of its way. When he saw Jack on the tram he stared at his blazer with the Presentation crest and looked from it to his own, the way you might compare two pennies to make out which one was the dud.

When they reached the school Jack leaped off the tram and ran up the side lane, shouting out 'Thanks, da . . . g'bye, now!' and leaving his da still on the platform, not knowing whether to follow him or to go to his work. Inside the school gate there was a concrete yard and a field, with tennis courts at the side. The older boys stood in twos and threes and talked; the new boys stayed by themselves close to the wall. Brother Berchmans walked from one group to the next, nodding and shaking hands while the wind lifted his cape into bat's wings. When he came to a new boy he stooped to him and said: 'Yah wahlcome.' Beyond the far wall, Jack saw the upstairs windows of a row of Corporation houses. He thought of the kind of people who lived there and how, here in Presentation, he was different from them from today out.

It was time to make a start. Flann Hartigen was talking to Denis O'Shaughnessy and another boy a few yards away. Jack walked over to them and stood listening, not putting in his prate but with the beginnings of a grin on his face for when they would speak to him. For a minute or so they paid him no heed, then, still without looking at him, Flann Hartigen said in his toff's accent: 'What a quaint old gentleman I see at the side gate.'

Jack turned around, ready to laugh at whoever it was, and saw his da peering in. When he caught Jack's eye he gave him a wave and a wink, then went marching off with smoke pouring from his pipe like from the crooked chimney of a tin shed.

'A horny-handed son of the soil, I would say,' Flann Hartigen said, his voice now louder. 'Do we know him? Do you, O'Shaughnessy?' Denis O'Shaughnessy spluttered high up inside his nose and looked at Jack. Flann Hartigen's eyes travelled along the look like two curtain rings on a rail. 'Ah!' he said to Jack as if he was charmed to see him. 'Good day to you. Perhaps the old gentleman belongs to *you*?'

He cocked an ear for an answer. The pink full moon of his face was politeness itself. Over his shoulder Jack saw two boys turning to look. He heard Brother Berchmans' voice saying to someone: 'This term, McGurk, we'll haff no slacking, if you plizz.' Flann Hartigen's face came nearer. 'Can't quite hear you,' he said. 'Do speak up. *Does* he belong to you?'

In a minute there would be a crowd around. He should have turned and walked away. But the shame and the shame of being ashamed swelled and spilled over inside him, so that he was more surprised than anyone to see his own fist ramming into Flann Hartigen's face, catching him on the soft underpart of the nose. He heard a boy shouting: 'There's a fight.' Out of the corner of his eye he saw Brother Berchmans' head swing around. The blow took his rage with it; hardly had it landed than he was shaking with fright, and all the more so when he saw that Flann Hartigen's eyes were bucketing tears of pain and that a red snot was bubbling out of his nose.

'Give over, lads,' someone said. 'Schnozz is looking.'

'You little gutty,' Flann Hartigen said in what was no longer a toff's voice. 'You wait.' He felt for the blood with the tip of his tongue and went off with Denis O'Shaughnessy and the other boy to what looked like the outside lav.

A Brother with a Kerryman's grin on his face appeared on the school step and rang a handbell. The boys started to move indoors. 'You'll be in Third Year, Kizz,' Brother Berchmans said to him, going by without stopping. His eyes began to smart. He had dreamed of doing the devil and all at Presentation; instead, it had taken him no more than five minutes to be shown up and disgraced for life, and then he had put the seal on it by hitting Flann Hartigen, a boy out of *The Magnet*. Even the worst sneaks and rotters in Greyfriars were not a patch on him. He thought of his da looking in at the side gate, and his face burned; but he had too much on his plate to start wondering whether he had been ashamed of him or for him.

Since today was the start of the school year there would be a half holiday. In the meantime, there were four lessons: Irish, Maths (in Harold Boys' School they had called it Arithmetic), Church History and Latin – the others had been learning Latin for a year past, so when he opened a book called *Gallic Wars* he might as well have been looking into a bush. At half-past twelve Brother Berchmans came in with a cardboard box under his arm.

'Ah haff bin esked by the parish prist,' he said, 'to hand aht some buks of raffle tickets in edd of the Purr of the Parish. Em sure that enny boy who calls himself a Catholic will lip at the opportunity of advancing a nobble coz.' He turned to Brother Alfred, who was the Latin teacher. 'Would you say we haff enny ticket-sellers present, Brother Alfred?'

'Oh, by the hokey we have,' Brother Alfred said, laughing while his eyes jumped from one boy to the next as if there was a secret pagan in the room.

Brother Berchmans took a batch of white tickets from the cardboard box. 'We shall soon find aht. Those boys who are ready to do God's holly work will raise their hens.'

Half the boys put their hands up straight off, then the others did the same in dribs and drabs, all but a dark grey-eyed boy in front of Jack. The only sounds in the room were the clock ticking and Brother Berchmans slapping the tickets slowly into the palm of his hand. 'We are waiting, Meldrum,' he said.

'No, thank you, Brother,' the boy said. His voice was cool.

Brother Berchmans' top lip went up until his teeth showed. 'You will not sell tickets?'

'No, thank you, Brother,' Meldrum said.

The Superior pointed at him. 'Then git aht of my sight!' The words came out like the spitting noise a cat would make.

'Yes, Brother.' Meldrum stood and walked out of the classroom, taking his time and closing the door softly behind him. A moment later they heard him whistling in the yard.

Brother Berchmans began to hand out the books of raffle tickets, starting at the front of the class and giving two to each boy. Jack awaited his turn; in his mind it was five minutes later and he was safely on the tram for Dalkey with this first terrible morning in flitters behind him. He reached out his hand for the tickets. Brother Berchmans made to give them to him, then stopped.

'No, Kizz,' he said. 'We don't want to be led into temptation.'

He moved on between the desks. It took Jack a full minute to realize why he had not been given tickets to sell. When the answer came, darting into his mind and out again, and finally settling, what surprised him most was his feeling of calm. He should have felt embarrassed or angry; instead he nearly smiled at the thought of how far away Greyfriars was.

Chapter 9

My great-aunt Julia lived in a ramshackle drunkard of a house on Sorrento Road. Hardly a year passed without part of the ceiling falling down in one room or another, and when the damage became severe enough she simply locked the door of the room in question and never set foot in it again. Years later, I was reminded of aunt Julia on seeing Graham Greene's play, *The Living Room*, in which two old women similarly abandoned any room in which someone had died.

I remember an old woman dressed in unending dusty layers of grey and black who called to our house one day and presented me with a mildewed copy of *Great Expectations* and then pushed a halfpenny into my hand with the unassailable observation that as long as I kept it I would always have money. My new affluence was short-lived, for she returned the following day to inform my mother that 'I want me bewk and me ha'penny, if ye please.' Aunt Julia was, of course, a genuine grey-blooded miser, and although she retrieved both the coin – or its likeness – and the book, the harm had been done. I had already travelled the marshes with Pip, stolen bread for Magwitch and nearly had a seizure when uncle Pumblechook drank the tar water. I was ten at the time, and years were to pass before I could again meet Joe Gargery and hold him to his glorious promise of 'Wot larks!' Which is a roundabout way of saying that the few pages I managed to read before aunt Julia had second thoughts marked the only time I ever caught myself in the process of being educated.

At Presentation College I learned next to nothing, and if I made not one lasting friendship in four years it was because, believing myself to be different, I became different. My initial efforts to be inconspicuous were so elaborate as to have the opposite effect, and I was for a time the prey of a small band of tormentors: sons of shopkeepers, insurance agents and dentists, and my own snobbery was fuel for theirs. One of them, a boy named Bertie Wright, now dead, used to follow me after school to see for himself the meanness of the cottage I lived in and report it gleefully next day to his cronies, and I led him for miles, through woods and farmyards, down cliffs and along the seashore: anywhere, except to Kalafat Lane. Being useless at fighting, I eventually learned to armour myself by cultivating a skill at deadly insult, usually and necessarily delivered as a Parthian shot. My success at excoriation was such that I became a crowd-pleaser, incapable of suppressing a well-turned jibe, no matter how dire the retribution.

Only one of the teaching staff was as class-conscious as the pupils, and that was the Superior: Schnozzle, as we called him. He alone among the community was not of peasant stock, and it was said that he had been forced into the religious life. Certainly, he was never happier than when entertaining mothers to tea and iced cakes in the parlour, batting his eyes at them, as arch as a coquette, and giggling like a convent girl. In the classroom he was a Torquemada. I can still remember the loosening of the bowels on hearing his flat nasal voice intoning the preamble to a caning: 'Git ahtside the door, pliss, Ah'll be aht in a minnit'; but the beatings frightened us less than the hatred of us we could sense behind his long coffin-shaped face with its smile like a cut throat. He had a fondness for the bottle, and during my final year he was transferred to the community house at Enniskillen, where the misfits, backsliders and rebels of the order were either rehabilitated or launched back into the outside world. Whether by his own choice or not, Schnozzle became laicized in due course and vanished from sight.

The most savage caning dealt out during my time at Presentation came not from the Superior but from Brother Alfred who taught Latin and religious knowledge. He was a Corkman: young, farmyard-handsome and popular: Patrick Pearse, had he been still alive, would have described him as clean-limbed. One day, while taking us for religious instruction, he talked about the power of prayer, how it never went unanswered and could achieve all things. When he had finished, Dinkie Meldrum put his hand up. It was Dinkie who, on my first day, had refused to be intimidated into selling raffle tickets. He was not a rebel: he simply went his own way. His indifference to what anyone else thought about him was monumental, and an unspoken truce seemed to exist between him and the Brothers: he would give them no trouble, provided he received none from them. He sat through each class meditating upon pictures of nudes he had cut out of *Lilliput* and kept between the pages of his schoolbooks, and for him to ask a question arising from a lesson was unprecedented. Brother Alfie's chest expanded a full inch on seeing his hand raised: he must have felt that he had achieved a breakthrough. 'Yes, Meldrum?'

'If you please, Brother,' Dinkie asked earnestly, 'surely prayers won't stop tanks or get you your breakfast?'

The same curiosity as to the likelihood of supernatural intervention in unspiritual matters was probably shared by most of the boys present, and I for one looked forward to a clarification from Brother Alfie. Instead, we saw his face turn a muddy red and his fists clench. He shook his head as if he had suddenly caught a whiff of decomposition. His speech seemed obstructed.

'That statement, Meldrum,' he said, 'is the very keystone of atheistic communism.'

He sprang at Dinkie, seized him, dragged him to the front of the class, took him by the wrist and began to cane him as if his hand had been firewood that needed chopping. 'I'll teach you communism,' he groaned as the cane whipped down. He had started on the other hand before Dinkie could believe it was happening to him and bellowed like a young bull: 'Let go of me, you bastard.' At this, Brother Alfie lost the last tatters of his self-control; he caught Dinkie by the scruff of the neck and, for what seemed like minutes, slashed at the backs of his legs. Frank McGurk, a crony of Dinkie's, stood up from his desk and said feebly: 'Ah, now ... ah, now ...', but otherwise none of us moved. At last the cane splintered and they came apart like exhausted fighters. 'Bloody bastard,' Dinkie said. Brother Alfie threw down the broken cane and went out of the room, stumbling against the door-jamb.

All that day and the next, the schoolyard was a gabble of excitement. Dinkie's hands and legs were covered with welts, and in a few places blood had been drawn. The fate of Brother Alfie was debated endlessly: he would be suspended, sacked, sent to Enniskillen, prosecuted, have the lard beaten out of him by Dinkie's father. To our dismay, however, none of these delicious possibilities came to pass: the official view of the incident was that Alfie had nipped an outbreak of incipient atheism in the bud. He became an acclaimed defender of the faith; Schnozzle even took him for a kind of lap of honour around the school field at lunch time, the pair of them arm in arm like sweethearts. What was worse, Dinkie's charmed life came to an end. Hitherto, he had been a black cat whose path no one dared cross; now, the Brothers and lay teachers alike made up for past remissness. He was moved from the back of the class to the front; he was singled out for special attention and given extra homework; he was caned almost daily. We had always had the vague belief that his aloofness was a sign of unused mental powers far in advance of our own; now we discovered that he was a woeful dud, incapable of subtracting x from $2x$. We had been betrayed: it was the fall of Parnell all over again.

He bore his misfortunes without complaint for perhaps six weeks, accepting the canings with his usual indifference, but his calmness fooled us no longer. Then one day, during a lesson in Catholic History, Brother Alfie decided that Dinkie was wool-gathering.

'Meldrum, stand up.' Dinkie stood. 'Summarize the lesson so far.'

'Pardon?'

The cane twitched in Alfie's hand. He had been more frightened than anyone by his frenzy of more than a month ago; he was by nature easygoing, but to be lenient now would be to own himself in the wrong.

'What,' he asked, 'were the chief obstacles to the rise of Catholicism in nineteenth-century America?'

Dinkie thought for a moment, then across his face the sun came up. 'Injuns,' he said.

Alfie lunged at him, but this time Dinkie was too fast. He ducked, ran, reached the door and was through it, taking the key with him. It slammed in Alfie's face and we heard the grating noise of the lock.

While Alfie pulled, pounded and shouted we stood on our desks and caught a last glimpse of Dinkie through the tall windows. Hands in trousers pockets, he ambled into the lane singing a scatalogical song of the period, which went to the tune 'Blaze Away':

'Bollicky Biddy
Had only one diddy
To feed the baby on.
Poor little fucker
Had only one sucker
To grind his teeth upon.'

In an attempt to keep burglars out and boys in, the windows had been doctored so that they opened no more than a few inches at the top and bottom, and it was an hour before a handyman came to release us by removing one of the frames. We were lowered down one by one to cheers from the assembled school, and Brother Alfie, like a ship's captain, was the last to leave, scrambling out to a mass whistled accompaniment of 'Blaze Away'. As for Dinkie it was the last any of us ever saw of him.

There were two lay-preachers: one, a retired sergeant-major who took us for physical training and believed that any boy, such as myself, who was less than a born athlete was not only a slacker but innately evil. Happily, I have forgotten his name, but the other teacher was Mr McLaughlin: a Northerner who, because of a slight ocular irregularity, was nicknamed Squinty. He was a bachelor, balding and with what I realized long afterwards was a perpetual whiskey tan. We thought of him as being well into middle age, but he was probably no older than forty. He knew everything about maths except how to impart his knowledge, and he was equally hopeless at keeping order in the classroom. He ranted, banged on his desk and threw the duster and bits of chalk at us, but it was not in his nature to use a cane or his fists, and, instinctively, we knew it. He had not the knack of cultivating a protective outer shell as the Brothers did; what we saw was raw and vulnerable, and we made the most of it, mimicking his accent and imitating his squint. His occasional attempts at humour were pleas for an armistice; he craved respect, and we withheld it because to deny him gave us a sense of power.

Not surprisingly, he drank like a fish in the evenings, alone in the Coliemore Hotel. A rumour went around that he had met a girl and that the pair of them had been seen walking on the sea front with a yard of space between them, shyness making Squinty's face glow even more than usual. If it was true, the courtship came to nothing, for late one night he fell from the third-floor window of his lodgings. The official story was that he had overbalanced while attempting to close his bedroom curtains. There were those, of course, who said otherwise: that the girl had refused him and the last spark of his instinct for survival had guttered out. If that was so – if he had died by design – we in his classroom had played our own small part.

My favourite among the Brothers was Seraphim, who bore an extraordinary resemblance to Boris Karloff. He was in his sixties and suffered from a kind of palsy which caused his head to nod perpetually like a toy dog in the rear window of a car. He taught Irish from necessity and English from choice. He believed that Prince Hal was the noblest character in all of Shakespeare: a paradigm of virtue, in whom chivalry, valour, princeliness and a total absence of side were gloriously combined. While convalescing from a bout of 'flu and still too weak to teach, Seraphim one day tottered into the classroom where his locum, Brother Athanasius, was furthering our acquaintanceship with *Henry IV, Part One*. 'Don't mind me, Brother,' he cackled, collapsing into a chair. Athanasius was furious at the intrusion. They were mortal enemies. If there had ever been a reason for their mutual detestation, no one now knew it; but two old mothers-in-law sharing the same kitchen could not have so begrudged each other the time of day. Whenever it was necessary for them to be together in public, Athanasius displayed an icy disdain, whereas Seraphim was master of the sly dig disguised as a pleasantry; and now he had invaded the classroom to taunt his enemy with his presence.

One of Seraphim's keenest regrets was that he talked through his nose, while Athanasius had a fine voice and could declaim verse with an orotundity which would have been envied by such an actor as Anew McMaster, whom we had seen the previous year in *Macbeth* tearing the scenery of the Gate Theatre to shreds. Today, with Seraphim sitting behind him, he embarked on Hal's soliloquy, beginning:

> I know you all and will awhile uphold
> The unyok'd humour of your idleness;

and, as usual, he made a meal of it. He snarled and cooed in the same breath; in his bass notes bitterns boomed, in his sibilants adders hissed; one hand plucked down pieces of firmament, while the other, under our noses, was an upturned claw. Throughout the performance, Seraphim kept trying to shake his head, as if he were a drama critic watching the world's worst actor, but his affliction caused him to nod at the same time, so that what we saw was a weird broken-necked motion. Athanasius concluded the soliloquy with a *coup de théâtre*; his voice cawed like a rookery at sunset, and he made a downward corkscrewing motion with one forefinger, the while causing his left eyebrow to ascend half-way up his forehead. It was John Barrymore to the life. He paused, giving us time to recover from the magnificence of it, then addressed the class.

'Of course,' he said, 'the same Hal was a consummate hypocrite.'

At this vilification of the saintly Prince Henry, we all gaped at Seraphim, whose chair seemed to have become electrified.

'All this blather about him mending his ways,' Athanasius went on, 'is arrant nonsense. The blaggard was glorying in his own squalor, having his cake and eating it by doing one thing and saying another. A typical two-faced Englishman: carousing with Falstaff one minute and backbiting him the next.'

By now Seraphim was on his feet. Still feeble after his illness, he went staggering sideways, so that the finger he had started to point at Athanasius ended up by indicting a statue of St Anthony.

'You ruffian,' he said. 'You ignorant ruffian.'

Athanasius could as soon have believed that the words were intended for the saint. It was the eleventh commandment that Brothers never disagreed among themselves in front of the common enemy, the boys; and to see one of them actually hurling abuse at another was like having a front-row seat at the end of the world. While Athanasius was still dumb from shock, Seraphim fired a second salvo, now shaking as much from rage as from palsy.

'How dare you,' he said, 'impugn the reputation of a saintly man? How dare the brazen likes of you besmirch the innocence of these boys with your allegations?'

Athanasius's face was the colour of snow in a coal yard. 'My dear Seraphim,' he whispered, 'control yourself.'

'You ignorant thooleramawn,' Seraphim said, slapping his hands together like an old tinker woman in a rage.

'Ho, ho, ho,' Athanasius said, giving us a death's-head grin, 'the boys will think you're in earnest.'

'You know as much about the works of William Shakespeare,'

Seraphim said, 'as my B.T.M. knows about snipe-shooting.'

We stared at them, our heads turning from side to side as if we were watching a tennis match played by madmen. The grin of Athanasius's face crumpled and died. 'You're a disgrace to your cloth,' he said.

'Do you tell me?' Seraphim said with pretended horror. He threw up his hands. 'Oh, goodness gracious, Athanasius!' A whinny of rapture went up from the class, which inspired him to favour us with an encore. 'Goodness gracious, Athanasius!' he chanted, his adenoids lending a new dimension to what was already a full-blooded sneer.

By now, Athanasius was shaking in a manner to outdo Seraphim. 'I am going to report you,' he wept.

'How audacious, Athanasius!' Seraphim sang, and we fell about like drunkards.

'To the Superior General,' Athanasius cried, adding rather mysteriously, if one considered Seraphim's age, 'You pup, you.'

At this, Seraphim picked up the duster from its place under the blackboard and, holding it between finger and thumb as if it were a dead rat, shook it in Athanasius's face. A fine cloud of blue and red chalk dust descended upon his hair and cassock. He backed away from Seraphim like an archaeologist in a horror film who has opened the forbidden sarcophagus. 'God save us,' he moaned, 'you're raving mad.'

He felt behind him for the door knob, found it, turned it and was gone. Seraphim all but pounded his chest in triumph. He smirked, snorted, stuck his tongue hard into his cheek to keep it from mischief and absent-mindedly wiped his face with the duster, so that coloured tears ran down his face. When he at last recovered his composure he turned to us. 'Now, boys,' he said, starting to wheeze, 'let me tell you about Prince Hal...'

One of the reasons that I liked Seraphim was that my hobby was drawing and he was a caricaturist's delight. His profile was that of a ruined Adonis; he had straight iron-grey hair and a roller-coaster of a nose; the furrows in his forehead and cheeks were cart tracks, and his Adam's apple leaned like a drunkard on the rim of his Roman collar. One day during a class break I dashed off an uncommonly good likeness of him on the blackboard in white chalk, gilding the lily with a drop of moisture on the end of his nose. For some reason, I went out into the schoolyard without remembering to erase the drawing, and when the bell went and we filed back into the classroom for the Irish lesson I saw to my dismay that Seraphim was standing in front of the blackboard, which had been wiped clean. I wondered if he had identified the caricature as of himself and, what was more to the point, if he could identify the artist.

The lesson had almost run its course and our ears were cocked for the jangling of the lunch bell when Seraphim took it into his head to give us examples of a particular Irish idiom. *'Thug sé asacháin dhuit,'* he droned, then translated: 'He has insulted you.' His hooded grey eyes alighted unmistakably on me and the nodding of his head increased in tempo. *'Thug tú asacháin dhom,'* he said; 'You have insulted me.' It was a reproach and – because his mouth was twitching – an absolution, both at once.

My academic career was a non event. The spurt of energy which had won me the scholarship soon fizzled out, perhaps because of my realization, kindled and nurtured by Brother Berchmans, that wherever I belonged it was nowhere near Presentation. Such was my apathy that I accomplished the feat of languishing in Fourth Year for three years running until the scholarship expired. I would simply stroll into my old classroom on the first day of the new autumn term and sit at my accustomed desk, and apart from a startled look from Seraphim at seeing me still there as if fossilized, I was paid no more attention than was accorded to the holy statues in their niches around the walls. My mother, however, seemed to regard this condition of suspended animation as a kind of honour, as if I were a variety artist who had been held over by public demand. 'Jack is in the same class again this year,' she would announce to her cronies, adding with a tight simper of pride: 'All the others was shifted.' Such proclamations were greeted by her listeners with loud panegyrics to my genius and her saintliness in rearing me. I was great, so I was, and a credit to her, and signs on it she was having her reward and more power to her. In time, I came to suspect that she was not so much innocent as crafty, for she took care not to boast of my academic *tour de force* to Chris and John, who were far less gullible than the old ones on our road. 'Don't say yes, aye or no to either of them,' she warned me. 'We don't want every dog and divil knowing our business.'

I left Presentation without a backward glance. Seven years later, I received a letter from the Superior asking if I would direct the boys in a Christmas programme of one-act plays. Brother Berchmans had long since left the order, Seraphim had retired from teaching and was drifting like a wraith from one community house to the next, and the few Brothers remaining from my time seemed to have shrunk physically. Instead of ageing, it was as if they had changed back into country lads. Innocence shone from them. I came upon Brother Joseph in the yard, pouring water over a patch of concrete. He was the youngest of them and giggled like a nun.

'I tell oo,' he said to me in a Cork accent as thick as dripping, 'if it freezes tonight we'll all be shliding till dawn!'

It did freeze, and under the December moon, as cold and yellow as a cat's eye, I saw yesterday's tyrants go slipping and spilling across the yard, looking in their black robes like witches on an outing. A few evenings later, the same Brother Joseph got into a car someone had parked in the yard, and Brother Alfie promptly stood in front of it imitating a policeman on point duty while Joseph made engine noises and tugged at the steering wheel and gear lever. In his excitement, however, he turned on the ignition, and the car leaped forward, hit Alfie and sent him flying. The two of them staggered into the house, weak from laughing, and the sight of Alfie's blood dappling the carpet only set them off all over again.

After rehearsals, the Superior would offer me a bottle of stout in the parlour. It was like receiving a certificate of manhood. He was a Kerryman, bubbling with good humour, and one evening as we talked he mentioned that he had been destined for the religious life from the age of twelve. I murmured something about how remarkable it was to have a vocation at such an early age. He let out a roar of laughter.

'Vocation, is it?' he said. 'Listen to me, boy, and come here till I tell you. Between the whole family of us at home we hadn't a ha'penny piece to bless ourselves with. Compared with us, Job's ass was a plutocrat. Seven children, and no hope for a one of them except England maybe or the fields. Then one day didn't this Presentation Brother come to the school and have a talk with the master – nosing out which of us were the brainy ones. Well, if I wasn't top of the class, I was rarely far from it, and that evening he comes out on the master's bicycle to talk to my parents.

' "Do you think," he asks them, "would young Martin here go to be a Brother in the Presentation?" And with that he dangles the carrot: a free education until I'm eighteen. "Then," he says, "if the lad decides not to come to us we won't lift a finger or say a word. Sure what good would he be to us if he wasn't cut out for the life?"

'Well, 'twas more than I'd ever dreamed of: a chance to get on in the world; and sure the mother was delighted, thinking she'd have the next best thing to a priest in the family. So off I go, nearly not able to walk with the weight of the holy medals from every house in the village, and I'm at boarding school for six years. During my last term the Superior sends for me. "Well," he says, "have you decided to stay with us?" It seemed a bit ungrateful to say "No" right into his face, so I shuffled my feet and told him I wasn't sure yet. "Indeed," says he, "I'd be worried if you *were* sure. Aren't you only eighteen?"

'He puts an arm around my shoulder. "Listen," he says. "We won't spoil the house for a lick of paint. We'll see you through the University, and at the end of the story if you decide to give us the go-by, sure what odds? It's happened to us before and 'twill again, and the bit of education will do you no harm."

'So off with me to Cork in a new navy-blue suit, and they paid for that, too. Boys, oh boys, I thought, I'm set up for life: with a degree in my fist there'll be no stopping me. Well, you can guess what happened. I went from college to the seminary; my final vows were three weeks off and I still couldn't get up the nerve to tell them that I hadn't a notion in the wide world of becoming one of them. Every day I said: I'll do it tomorrow. Of course I never did. And here I am now.'

The Superior took my glass and opened another bottle of stout. He had the grin of a cat.

'Vocation, how are you!' he said. 'Would you ever get yourself stitched, boy!'

Chapter 10

The sun was splitting the trees and he had the front door on the hinge when his ma said not to go out until he had written the letter to Mrs Pim.

His da had been given a pension of ten shillings a week when Mrs Jacob died, and every three months there would come the cheque for six pounds ten and a letter written on blue paper with wording of a darker blue that said *Annegrove, Mountmellick, Co. Westmeath*. The letter hoped that they were all keeping well and was signed *Winifred R. Pim*. Mrs Pim was the Jacobs' daughter, and sometimes when she came to Dublin for the day she would call to the house and sit in the baldy armchair by the range, saying: 'How are you, Keyes, and how is our dear Enderley?' His da was still working there, for the new owners who were Catholics, and the name of the house was Santa Maria now, but of course to him it was Enderley for ever more. The new people and himself were oil and water: for one thing, they had an ordinary way of talking – not like the quality at all; for another, they followed him around the garden to make certain that he earned his four pounds ten a week and was not idling in the greenhouse or the stable loft. 'Never work for your own,' he would tell Jack, 'for they'd skin you.' And with Mrs Pim forenenst him, holding a cup of tea in one hand and a cut of buttered brack in the other, he would go rawmayshing about the old days, a sob rising in his throat when he mentioned the Master and the Mistress, sure God be good to them. She said 'Indeed' or 'Dear me' every now and again to keep him happy, letting him talk the way you would let a dog run free in a park for a while. She wore a knitted cap with a tassel the size of your fist, and her brown lisle stockings were stretched at the knees when she sat, so that the skin showed through. There was a scent off her you could not place, a smell of gardens. When she spoke, every word was kept distinct and on its own, the way you would divide a bar of chocolate into fair shares. She had never stuttered or whispered in her life.

When she had given his da his say for long enough, she would interrupt him, turning to Jack. 'I hope,' she said, 'that when you find employment and make your own way in the world, you will be good to this old man.'

'Oh, Jack's the lad won't see us stuck,' his da said, and the thought of Jack being good to him brought a second lump into his throat, clattering against the first one like a hacking chestnut.

Jack's ma did not say yes, aye or no to this, but her eyes went darker and her mouth smaller. She had never forgiven Mrs Pim for the spectacle frames from the San Francisco earthquake or for the twenty-five pounds lump sum. Later, when their visitor had taken herself off to Mountmellick, leaving a whiff of lavender in the kitchen and the scent of verbena in the hall, Jack's da would be skewered with a look for letting himself be called an old man.

'The cheek of her,' his ma would say, 'with her ten shillings a week and then coming in here and being pass-remarkable. Her and her "old man" out of her. I wouldn't like to be hanging since she passed fifty.'

A week before the cheque was due, she would be on the lookout for Dick Cullen, the postman, and if the first of the month went by and it had not come there would be a face on her like a plateful of mortal sins. 'Bad scran to her, that money is dead,' she would say angrily, meaning that it was already spent or as good as, on shoes for Jack or a winter coat for his da or new wallpaper for the kitchen, for she was the devil for style. Then, just when she was about to call Dick Cullen a robber to his face, the envelope was slid under the weatherboard of the door.

'There now, Mag,' his da would say, and now of course she would pretend that it was no matter to her whether the money had ever been sent or no. 'We've been so long waiting for it,' she would grumble, 'that all the good has been took out of it.'

It was Jack's job to write to Mrs Pim to thank her, if only, his ma said, to show her that they were in the land of the living and had manners every bit as good as her own. Today was Sunday, when he and his friend Oliver would go down the sea front in Dun Laoghaire, so when she called him back he sat at the kitchen table in a temper.

waiting while she put the notepad and the blue-black ink in front of him.

'Tell her that you're done with school,' she said, 'and please God she might find you something.'

She meant work. He had had a job only the once, two years ago when he was sixteen, as a French soldier in *Henry V* the time it was filmed above in Powerscourt. It was the Battle of Agincourt: he lay down and was a corpse one week and ran into a swamp and was drowned the next. Later, when he saw the film at the Pavilion, there were so many soldiers packed together and drowning that you could not see the swamp. It had been a great gas, except for getting your legs painted yellow or red to look like tights, but now of course he needed something steadier. He wrote: 'I am out of Presentation College this month past and like Mr Micawber am waiting for something to turn up.'

'What sort of codology is that?' his ma said when she read it.

'How?'

'*Who* is it you're like?'

'It's a character out of a book.'

The way he said it, short and sweet, told her she would not understand and that it would be a waste of his time to explain. It told her that she read books by Ruby M. Ayres and Nat Gould and that he was cleverer than she was. More than that, it told her that there was a foreign language he could speak that would be understood by Mrs Pim and not by her.

She said: 'Write it out again and do it proper.'

'What for?'

'Because I tell you to.'

He looked across at his da, who had the *Sunday Dispatch* open at the racing page and was wondering what ailed the pair of them. His mad aunt Mary was sitting at the kitchen table with her eyes turned up. 'Because he's told to, Mag,' she said.

'You dry up,' he said. Then, to his ma: 'There's this character who's an optimist –'

'I won't tell you a second time.'

'It's my letter. You're not writing it: I am.'

'Then do it proper.'

'Proper*ly*,' he said.

The old look came on her face: the one that said it was the price of her for rearing him. 'Don't you pull *me* up,' she said. 'Don't you act the gent with *me*, not in this house. They all said I'd rue the day, and gawm that I was I didn't believe them. Me own mother, me good neighbours –'

'Oh, play another record.'

'Don't you back-answer me, you cur. Showing off for the Pims, setting yourself up to be what you're not, no, and never will be ... they must have a right laugh at you.'

His face told her that if she had not hit the mark she had staggered it. 'A nice article to be let go to the Presentation, acting the man-een, letting on he's the quality, and the whole pack of them making a jeer of him.'

'Ah, Mag,' his da said.

'Sure you're not good enough for him either, no more nor I am.' Her small round body was shaking. She leaned against the table so that the edge of it cut into her. Her fists, pressed down on yesterday's *Irish Press* that was the tablecloth, were bunched and white. 'Well, thanks be to God,' she said, 'there's them in this house that knows where they were got and how they were got.'

It would be years before he learned that love turned upside-down is love for all that. Now, his hate was too much for her alone: it ran past her like a flood tide: it took in his da and Mary: it swallowed the room itself, the row of cracked jugs filled with betting slips and spools of thread, the bakelite grotto, turning from white to yellow, that said 'A Present from Lourdes', the old coats behind the door that were used as blankets on winter nights, the clock on the dresser, lying on its back like an invalid. Most of all, as the sea had done on the day his da tried to drown the dog, the hate filled his own eyes and mouth. He got up from the table, but his ma was at the door before him. 'You're not going from here until that letter is wrote.'

She had moved at such a lick of speed for her size that to his dismay he felt a grin come out of nowhere and he shot it for its treachery. He said: 'There's nothing wrong with it, and I'm not doing it again.'

'Oh, are you not?' She looked past him. 'Nick.'

'Ah, son,' his da said. 'Write it out again the way she wants you to.'

'Don't beg him,' she said. 'Tell him.'

At this, his da let a roar out of him that made Mary jump and say 'Jesus'. 'Will you do as you're bloody well told,' he said, 'and not be putting the woman into a passion? Can we not have peace in the house on a shaggin' Sunday without you and your curse-o'-God jack-actin'?'

The upshot was that he wrote the letter again, getting his own back by ending it with 'Yours, and oblige', as if it was a note to Toole's shop looking for tick. His da, beaming now, his temper gone like smoke from his pipe, stood over him and said: 'Begod, son, you always made a great fist of writing a letter.' His ma, coffined in her sulks, was limping around the kitchen to show how much he had taken out of her. He went to the door again, unhindered this time, and gave her daggers' looks. 'Mag, he's makin' faces,' said Mary the informer.

By the back road that dipped down into Glasthule and climbed out again as if policemen were chasing it, it was a mile and a bit to where Oliver lived in Crosthwaite Park. The sky burned and made his eyes ache; along Eden Road the tar shone and smelled new again. The trees were a tired August yellow-green, standing heavy as a glutton might, afraid to breathe until the fullness went. It was still dinner time: the roads were dozing. He whistled under his breath as he walked, thinking about the film *Lifeboat* he had seen last week at the Astoria. He had not forgotten the row with his ma: it had come with him like a dog to the corner of Begnet's Villas and would be waiting there when the last tram brought him home. *Lifeboat* had been brutal, a washout, but he remembered the bit where a man held up a newspaper and there was this advertisement for slimming, with one picture of Alfred Hitchcock real fat as 'before' and another one of him not so fat as 'after'. It was his way of getting into the film somehow, even though it all took place in this lifeboat. Jack had nudged the man sitting next to him. 'That's Alfred Hitchcock,' he said. 'Feck off,' the man said.

Oliver lived in the hall flat of the end house where, from the bay window, you looked across tennis courts. His mother was a fierce woman for moving. Previously, they had lived in Monkstown, and before that in Dalkey, on the Barrack Road. There, they played chess on the landing under the gap lamp and listened to the noises from the back room. They could see the door of this room from the stairs: it was kept shut and there were iron bars on the windows because it had once been part of the old police barracks next door. It was bare of furniture except for an iron bedstead, and yet every night there came these crashings, scrapings and thumpings, like from ten peluthered handymen.

'What is it?' Jack had asked the first time he heard it.

'Oh-there-you-have-me,' Oliver said in the loud, jolly, every-word-the-same voice he had used ever since he took the elocution lessons, and went on setting out the pieces on the chessboard.

Jack's first thought was that Oliver's da, Mr Mongan, was in the room, cod-acting to take a rise out of him. 'Do you see the green in me eye?' he said and ran up the half-flight, throwing open the door; but there was only the room, now quiet, with the shadows of the window bars flung slantwise across the floor by the street lamp on Railway Road. In time, he became as used to the noises as Oliver was: they would yell out 'This is Funf speaking' or sing 'Open the door, Richard!'; but whenever the gas light began to blink and die they would be down the stairs and out of the house like whippets, not coming back until someone – Oliver's mother or his da or his aunt who lived with them – put a shilling in the meter. One night, there was a noise worse than any knockings or bangings. They heard music and singing: far off, muffled and crackling, like an old gramophone.

Whatever was in the room or was not, people said that Oliver's mother was the cause of it. She had won a mint of money – five hundred pounds – in a crossword competition, and it had turned her peculiar: talking your head off one day and biting it off the next. She would queen it into the pork shop or Findlater's or the Leinster House as if she was the quality calling upon tinkers, and tell them they were robbers trying to diddle her, and, sign's on it, she was having them deported. Once, she pushed Oliver's aunt half-way out of an upstairs window, and all that saved the poor woman was that Mrs Mongan let go of her while she went to look for a hatchet. If you asked how any of this could connect her with the nightly concert in the back room, you would be smiled at for your innocence and told that the devil's children have the devil's luck and if you want to know me come and live with me. In the heel of the hunt, howsomever, the know-it-alls were wrong, for when the Mongans moved to a flat in Monkstown the noises still went on. In fact, after a night in the back room one of the new tenants swore a hole in an iron pot that he had seen an old woman stepping over his bed, and before that week was out the whole town turned up to see Father Creedon saying prayers over the house.

'Ah, yass, a grand and glorious Irish evening,' he said to anyone who saluted him as he sailed down Castle Street at the head of a procession of no one. He had a holy water bucket in one hand, a sprinkler, shaped like a drumstick, in the other and prayer book under his oxter. The crowd around the front door made way for him and a woman said 'God protect you, Father.' He gave her his blessing, forgetting that he was holding the sprinkler, and in a second she looked like a watered fuchsia. He hung the holy water bucket on the crook of his arm as if it was a handbag and opened his prayer book. The way he blessed himself made the people next to him step back for fear of being hit, treading on the feet of whoever was behind them, and his voice sang out over the slate roofs: 'In NOMine PAAHtrie et FILii et SPIRituuus SAHNCTi ... AHHHmen.' Then, dipping the sprinkler and waving it, he made a bull's rush through the doorway of Number 28 and was gone from sight. He was wearing his altar slippers and the only sound was the smack of the holy water hitting the stairs. There was silence then, except, now and again, for the far-off thunder of his praying. A few of the old ones in the crowd had their beads out and were wading through the Sorrowful Mysteries; the others were quiet, hoping for something to happen and afraid that it might. After a while, a young lad in a red gansy – a little gouger from White's Villas up the town – edged to the open front door and slipped inside. Before anyone could make a move to go in after him, he was out again with a face that would frighten you. 'Jasus, run,' he said. 'It's comin' out.'

It was the 'it' that did the damage. He could have shouted 'He's comin' out' or 'She's comin' out'; but no, the little gett said 'it', and where there was a crowd one minute there was a stampede the next. Johnny Quinn, who was sitting on the window sill of the Foresters' Hall, that used to be the police barracks, was butted in the chest and fell backwards into the committee room, taking the window with him, and poor old Winnie Carthy that kept the sweetshop was knocked down and stepped on. When Father Creedon came out of the house after doing his praying and having a cup of tea in his hand to be sociable, there was not a cricket stirring except for the young lad that had started the rush, and Johnny

Quinn, who was crying in the Foresters' Hall. He looked up and down the empty road and patted the young lad on the head and gave him sixpence. 'Couldst thou,' he said to the crowd, even though it was a mile away by now and still travelling, 'not watch with me one hour?'

The only noises from the back room of the flat where Oliver lived now, in Crosthwaite Park, were of his father snoring. He was a bus driver and because he talked through his nose like a black he was nicknamed Sammy. Himself and Mrs Mongan did not get on. Between him and Oliver there was never a cross word, but he was like a man who kept from tricking with what he did not understand, and believed that even God Almighty would draw the line at trying to understand Oliver. Now, while Jack was still on the front steps, he opened the door. He was wearing his busman's uniform with the silver watch-chain. 'Ollie,' he shouted down the hall, 'Kokomoko is here.' He gave Jack a wink to show that there was no harm in the name and went down the steps, singing through his nose and happy to be away from the person he could not understand, as well as from the other person that he could.

Oliver came into the hall in his shirt sleeves and fastening his tartan tie. 'Sappy days,' he said.

'Sappy days,' Jack said. It was a saying they had.

He told Oliver that it was roasting out and there would be a mob on the pier. 'Oh-jolly-good,' Oliver said and went off again to get ready. Because Jack was not invited into the flat he knew that Mrs Mongan was either as cross as two sticks or in one of her silences where if you talked to her she would turn her head away as if the wall made more sense to her than you did. He sat on the front step, bursting the blisters of green paint on the hall door and listening to the slow pock of a tennis ball from across the way.

When it came to getting ready to go out, you might as well order the sun to set early as try and hurry Oliver. He would take twenty minutes to wash himself, another ten foosthering with the knot in his tie and five more tugging at the handkerchief in his breast pocket until it sprouted like a flower. He had two handkerchiefs: for show and blow. 'Always look after your appearance,' he said once, 'and pronounce properly. That's how you get on.' His suit never had a speck on it, and there was a crease in his trousers you could pare a pencil on. He filed his nails, then polished them. He rubbed Silvikrin into his hair, which was dark and in neat waves except for one strand he left hanging loose on purpose, as if he was Charles Starrett, maybe, after a fight with the bully.

The time his mother won the five hundred pounds she had taken him out of the national school, meaning to send him to the Christian Brothers' secondary; then, the contrary sort she was, she changed her mind. That was when he was twelve and he had not been to school since. He was not worried: you would never be stuck, he said, as long as you developed your personality. Learn to be masterful and there would be no stopping you. So he sent off for the Charles Atlas course and did the exercises, even giving himself cold friction rubs, whatever *they* were. He went to Potter's College to learn elocution, and now he talked like a bacon slicer, using the same voice to let you know you had won the Sweep as he would to tell you your dog was run over. He was teaching himself psychology out of books you would strain yourself lifting. ' "I think, therefore I am",' he said to Jack. 'That's from Des Carty.' His favourite book of all was called *How to Win Friends and Influence People*, and he could spout screeds from it. He was doing Pelmanism so as to be magnetic, and lately he had joined the Rosicrucians, which brought out your hidden powers. This was secret stuff, but he told Jack about the Cathedral of the Soul and how he had meditated and lit rose-scented candles in front of a looking glass and had seen his face changing to what it had been like in previous existences. 'Oh-very-frightening-you-know,' he said.

The lads on the sea front thought that Oliver was a howl. 'The guy has flipped his lid,' Dan Cleary said, throwing a piece of invisible popcorn into the air, catching it in his mouth like Alan Ladd did in *The Blue Dahlia* and giving a sad Richard Conte smile out of his Glenn Ford face. Joe Byrne agreed with him, saying that Oliver was a proper head-the-ball, but Liam Cooney said no, that he was more of a harmless gobshite. Whichever he was, eejit or head case, they were careful not to laugh too loud or too long. Dan and Liam were apprentices, one to a watchmaker, the other to an electrician, and Joe helped his cousin Pat, who mended shoes. They could see their lives running straight in front of them, cut and dried, and knew that they could no more change direction now than the Dalkey tram could turn and go up the mountains. But Oliver was still at the starting gate, biding his hour so quiet and calm that you half-expected him to make a leap and maybe go haring past the lot of them. Then it would be they who would be the gobshites.

You could not ask for better company. He would laugh, nod and be agreeable, never arguing the toss, but saying: 'By-Jove-you're-right-you-know', and then, so gently that you had to think twice to notice it, go his own sweet way. He would share out his cigs, lend you a bob till Friday for the pictures or a table in the billiard hall and listen to your troubles with never a yawn: and yet, the more obliging he was, the more you felt a grudge against him that swelled and turned white like a boil. You could endure a messer or a hook or a bollix, even, but what you could not forgive in Oliver was the worst lousiness of all – he had no need of you.

It was true. You could put him in your pocket but never own him. The lads and Jack were like a row of cottages, each one held up by the next and with one wall shared, but Oliver was a house standing off on its own, and whether he was too clever to need people or too thick, you could never be sure. If you found an excuse to have a row with him he would give his high-voiced laugh and remember he had a heavy date with Betty Brady or Maureen O'Reilly, saying: 'Must-be-hitting-the-old-trail ... the-wife-you-know.' Then he was off along the sea front with that half-dancing walk of his, as if he had a spring in him. He was like a bubble in a piece of oil cloth: push on him and he went someplace else.

He was a desperate man for the women. Betty Brady, who had come over from England on account of the war, was mad about him and so jealous that she could hear a wink. She was sixteen years old, but you would give her another three, and from the way she linked him into the Pavilion or the Picture House you knew she was a red-hot coort. Still and all, one evening she moaned to Jack about how Oliver had put his hand on her chest during Maria Montez in *Cobra Woman*. She was not worth her salt from the shock of it, and the part of her Oliver was supposed to have touched was pumping like a bellows.

'Oh, Jack,' she said. 'I thought he had respect for me. And I just sat there and let him. I was petrified. Oh, God, where will it stop, now that I've encouraged him?'

Jack could not answer. He was staring bug-eyed at her chest, trying to imagine it without the fawn-coloured coat, the pullover, the blouse, the woolly vest and whatever else. The only dynamite coort he had ever had was off a dark girl with the nickname of Sticky Taite, and that was in a laneway near York Road. He had walked her home, then chanced his arm, rushing at her like a bull at a gate and landing a kiss that barked his nose off hers. It was over before he realized that her lips were different from other girls': instead of being soldered together, with the teeth clamped shut like iron bars behind red curtains, they had given way to him. As he drew back from her she smiled, reached out and said: 'C'm'ere to me.' Her arms went slowly around him, her legs opened and fastened on his thigh, her mouth ate him. It occurred to him where she had got her nickname, for between him and her from the knees up you could not have stuck a page from a penny copybook. Half an hour later, he went to meet the lads in the Roman Cafe, his heart thudding, the legs buckling under him and the sweet heavy taste of lipstick in his mouth.

When he told Liam Cooney about how Oliver had put his hand on Betty Brady's chest, Liam laughed and said: 'Will you go 'long out of that. He wouldn't know what to do with a diddy if she took it out and waved it at him.'

'No, honest. She was shaking.'

'Yeah, from wanting it and not getting it. There's more goes on inside that one's head than ever went on further down. If Mongan laid a finger on her he'd be in Lourdes now, praying for his hand to drop off. And you, you sap, you believed her.'

It made sense. Oliver was a great man for self-control: according to the Rosicrucians, he said, to be master of others you must first be master of yourself. Often, the lads would come the heavy, nudging him and winking: 'Eh, Ollie, did you ever get a bit? Come on, tell us ... did-ja, wha'?' Oliver would take it in good part. 'Oh-now,' he would say, 'that would be telling. Ho-ho.' He believed that the greatest quality you could find in a girl was to be sincere, and he and Jack had made a list of all the sincere girls in the town, or at least on the sea front. Besides, he modelled himself on Tyrone Power, who was married to Annabella, and *Picturegoer* said they were Hollywood's happiest couple, preferring to spend their evenings in their cosy Bel Air home instead of becoming part of the studio colony's glamorous social whirl. Even in films, Tyrone Power might start off as a right louser, like in *Johnny Apollo* or *Crash Dive*, but he always redeemed himself in the end, and the most he gave Anne Baxter or Betty Grable was an old kiss and no messing. 'Of course, I know it's not true to life,' Oliver would say, 'but the thing is, it gives you ideals-you-know.'

Jack had punctured every blister on the hall door before Oliver was done titivating himself. They walked down into the town, talking about films the length of Mulgrave Terrace and Marine Road until the pier came in sight. It was bright with the colours of summer frocks: what you noticed most were the reds and yellows, either moving towards the bandstand or like quiet bunting on the benches or the folding chairs you paid fourpence for. Along the sea front there were the smells of scent and sea-wrack. Today, the pier seemed to have a lighthouse at each end, for where it began the sun flashed off a great hill of bicycles – a hundred near enough – thrown tangled together after the journey out from Dublin, crawling the hot winding length of the Merrion Road while the trams sang past them.

Jack and Oliver walked down the pier along the lower level. Among the people on the chairs above them, a woman was sitting with her ankles crossed and knees spread wide, her long pale-green knickers saluting the day. Jack looked away quickly and nudged Oliver, who turned in time to see the knickers vanishing as her knees shut like a trap. 'Oh-now,' he said, going red, and went on about the film censor and what a louser he was to cut out all the bits of *Reveille with Beverly* where Ann Miller showed her legs. The mention of legs reminded them of the women in the passion killers and they went into kinks. 'No-it's-too-blooming-hot,' Oliver said, and that only made it worse, for it was another saying of theirs, which they had heard William Lundigan say in *The Sea Hawk*.

Near the bandstand, they met Maureen O'Reilly and the ugly girl she knocked around with. Maureen was plump, with fair hair and nun's eyes, flirting with the ground she walked on. She and Oliver had been doing a steady line ever since last April when the war was nearly over and Betty Brady had been dragged back to London bawling her eyes out. From her permed hair down to her shiny dark nylons and high heels she was as neat as a bandbox and out of the same pod as Oliver: seeing them together, you would take them for two dummies that had stepped down out of Lee's window to go for a walk. Betty Brady had not been the worst of them: for all her codology, you could give her a squeeze whenever Oliver was at home learning how to be magnetic, and not only would she squeeze back but not go carrying tales. As far as Maureen O'Reilly was concerned, however, Jack and the lads were back of the neck: a coarse element, she called them. One evening on the pier, Liam had said: 'Hey, Maureen, is it true you're Oliver's new wife-you-know?' She had walked on, then turned back to them. 'Oliver is too soft,' she said. 'He lets your kind make free with him, and the only reward he gets is to be jeered at.'

They watched her heels typing a goodbye message to them on the granite flags. She had given them a right lemoner and it took Liam a minute to get over it. 'Talk about having a smell of yourself,' he said. 'That one thinks she pees lemonade.'

Dan Cleary flicked a finger at the snap brim of his hat and smiled sleepily. 'The broad has lost her marbles,' he said.

Today, she was wearing a gipsy sort of blouse that showed off her shoulders. 'Well-hell-o,' Oliver said with as much surprise as if he thought she had been in Fiji.

She gave the turn-ups of his trousers a pleased pink smile. 'Hello,' she said to them, 'isn't it shocking hot?'

'Oh-don't-be-talking,' Oliver said, quick as a flash.

She threw Jack a hello that fell on the pier and rolled into the harbour, then she and Oliver moved away and stood talking, with him giving her his You-are-in-my-power-but-I-will-spare-you-never-fear look and her whispering at him like in a confession box. Jack was left with her ugly friend, a girl called May Something, who had frizzy hair and a sour torn purse of a mouth. One day, he had been looking at her and thinking how desperate you would want to be to go with her, and at that moment he realized she was thinking the exact same about him. Since then, there had been the hatred between them of two people who are not good enough for one another. She looked straight through him at the three church spires of the town, and he looked through her at the bandstand. The Number 1 Army Band was playing 'Take a Pair of Sparkling Eyes.' The tune itself was as lilting as the day and the crowds, but the softness of the brass was melancholy, as if in regret for happy things that were gone.

Oliver finished his conversation and waved goodbye to Maureen, who went off down the pier with her stop-the-clock friend. A bunch of hard chaws from the town had their eyes glued to her bare shoulders, as pink as two legs of lamb. 'Are you seeing her later?' Jack asked.

'Oh-now,' Oliver said.

They found room to sit on the steps, hot under them, between the two levels and listened to the band. Off beyond the mailboat pier you could make out part of Dublin, lying like an old dog too hot to move. Jack began to sort what was left of the day into suits. Oliver's 'Oh-now' meant that he would be taking Maureen to the Pavilion after tea; they would sit at the back in the one-and-fourpennies, where the lads, below in the shilling seats, would not be near enough to blackguard them with 'Get your hand off that girl' or 'Eh, Ollie, would you risk it for a biscuit?' In the meantime, Jack could not go home to Oliver's house for tea because Mrs Mongan was in the glooms, or to his own house on account of the row with his ma. In his pocket he had one and eleven pence. That was a shilling for the pictures and eightpence for a glass of milk and a ham sandwich, instead of a proper tea, at the Roman Cafe. Tonight, maybe he could touch his da for fivepence to go with the three d. that was over: that would be enough for *The Uninvited* tomorrow afternoon. He was okie-doke until Tuesday, so. He was steeped.

He looked at Oliver, who had spread a handkerchief – the one for blow – under him when he sat and was tapping one long forefinger, stained yellow from ciggies, in time with the band. Their time for being friends was nearly up. Maureen's pull on Oliver was stronger than Jack's: she would win the tug-o'-war – at least until the day came when she would pull at him too hard and find the rope hanging empty in her hand.

A stout woman named Miss McGuinness was on the bandstand singing 'I Dreamt that I Dwelt in Marble Halls'. Jack grinned, remembering the time the lads had sung it in the queue for the Pavilion and had been turfed out by Fleming the usher because the words they used were:

> I dreamt that I tickled my grandfather's balls
> With a drop of sweet oil and a feather.
> My grand-da, poor bugger, didn't like it at all,
> For his balls they went slap-bang together.

It was too hot to worry about Oliver. He found himself wondering if he would ever learn to seize a day like this, to use it somehow or keep it, instead of watching it go brushing past him into evening.

Chapter 11

I saw Oliver the other day. He might have been setting out for a date with Betty Brady in the autumn of 1943. He wore a blue tweed suit from Burton's and suede shoes; in his breast pocket a poinsettia-red handkerchief was in flower; his gloves were turned back at the wrists; his scarf, thrown once around his throat, drifted behind him like a pennant. He was as lean as a whippet and still had the jolting long-paced walk of a lad on his way to an adventure. The only sign of age was when the wind blew his hair forward, showing a patch of baldness and giving him the look of a gentile Disraeli.

He lives on a council estate and has never owned a car. Jobs keep collapsing under him. He is a rent collector one year, a dispatch clerk the next; he waits for the world to come to him and is unbothered when it does not. Whenever there are hard times and staff are laid off, Oliver is always the first to go because he already has his hat in his hand and his coat on. His wife is a charming person who is delighted to have married her own private matinée idol; they have a family. His only regret is that he never achieved his great ambition: to become a cinema manager and stand at the back of the stalls, a cynosure in dinner jacket and black tie, watching the same film three times a day. Once, a few years ago when such a job fell vacant, I succeeded in having him short-listed. 'This will be a great thrill for the wife-you-know,' he said, and then never turned up for the interview. I think, to use the Irish phrase, that he disliked being under a compliment. He is still jovial: everyone's friend and no one's. I met him in the Carnegie Library a month ago: he had four books on the occult and two on self-improvement. In a moment of confidence he told me that when Maugham's *The Razor's Edge* came out he recognized himself as Larry Darrell instantly. Nowadays, whenever I approach him at a bus stop, he will peer into the distance or a shop window so that I must be the one who speaks first: then he gives a great overdone start of delight and we are friends still. He never talks about the past and yet he never left it.

In Ireland the war years were known as 'the Emergency'. The term is petulant, somehow, as if it had been inspired by a newspaper headline saying: 'War in Europe, Africa and the Pacific – Ireland Gravely Inconvenienced.' The bread became darker and coarser and acquired laxative powers which increased as the war wore on, until by D-Day it had the efficacy of an enema. There was rationing, of course, but the worst privation of all was the allowance of a half-ounce of tea per person per week. Tea was the champagne of the poor, and my mother would spread the used leaves on the window sill to dry in the sun and be employed again and perhaps a third time, until what finally dribbled from the teapot was the colour of diluted lime juice. Private motoring was banned by law, and a friend of mine was given ten shillings to dismember a Rolls Royce and throw it piecemeal into the sea. The gas was turned off at the mains outside of peak hours, but you could still coax a flame the size of a rush-light and risk being disconnected if you were caught cooking on it: for there was a government inspector known as the Glimmer-Man who came knocking at doors and walked straight in to feel the warm burner where you had been heating up stirabout or a baby's bottle.

It was a grey and grey-faced time. There was a college for wireless operators in Limerick; my mother found the brochure I had sent for and tore it up, not worth her salt from fear. My father, according to himself, was pro-German, holding that Hitler was the greatest man – barring De Valera – that ever trod shoe leather. The truth of the matter was that he was anti-English and pro-nobody, but he could never grasp the distinction. 'Hitler,' he would say, 'oh, he's the boy will give them lackery.' At which he would trot out his litany about the Black-and-Tans and decent people being shot in their beds and how it was the mercy of God that his brother Johnny had escaped the time of the ambush on the Ulverton Road. My mother would look daggers at his IRA service certificate hanging framed by the door: his only reward for nearly getting the pair of them shot. 'Old gobshite,' she said to him. 'You'd give a body the sick.'

The nearest the war came to Ireland was when the Germans dropped bombs on Dublin, killing people on the North Strand.

Months later, I was watching *The Man in Grey* at the Pavilion when there was a series of bangs. It was caused by the firing-off of the gun at the lifeboat shed opposite, but the building shuddered and someone yelled: 'It's the Jerries again.' There was another bang that seemed to come from under the floorboards, and the audience leaped up and made for the exits, some by the aisles, others over the seats. As the place emptied like a sieve, I could hear the voice of the commissionaire, Fleming, above the curses and the moans of 'Oh, Mammy, Mammy'. He was standing at the back, supervising the stampede and intoning in a bored sing-song, as if announcing that there was standing room only in the one-and-fourpennies: 'Positively no readmission ... positively no readmission.'

I was a great joiner in those days. First of all, aged fourteen, I enlisted in the Emergency Communications Corps and was issued with a tin helmet, and armband and a wreck of a bicycle on which with the fleetness of Mercury I was expected to ferry dispatches between the ARP headquarters in Dalkey and Dun Laoghaire. Most bicycles have a free-wheel; this did not, and whenever I absent-mindedly attempted to coast down a hill the pedals would continue to turn, hoisting me out of the saddle and, on one occasion, into a nearby flowerbed.

Later, I joined the Local Defence Force, which was the Irish equivalent of the British Home Guard, and was duly fitted out in boots, leggings and a green uniform that hung on me like a sack on a sweeping brush. I never succeeded in passing the Test of Elementary Training, not through any fault of my own, but because, just as our platoon reached the end of the course, another raw recruit would arrive and back we would all go to the beginning. Our proudest moment was when eight hundred of us were conscripted into the British and French armies as foot soldiers and archers in Olivier's *Henry V*. We spent a glorious summer holiday under canvas, for which we each received four pounds ten shillings a week, and the country never knew how fortunate it was that the Germans did not launch an invasion while the flower of its armed forces were imitating the action of the tiger at Agincourt.

We were a lethargic group, and the army sergeant who taught us small-arms drill once a week in Dalkey town hall endured us as if he were on Calvary and we were his cross. One evening, just to see if it was within our power to move smartly, he pulled the pin from a dummy hand grenade, lobbed it into our midst as we sat drinking cocoa and stood back, watch in hand, to time how quickly the hall emptied. Many a promising military career was blighted during the next four seconds or so, but my own farewell to arms occurred some months later when I was killed on a night exercise.

The idea was that the 'enemy' – a rival unit from Bray – would attempt to break through our lines somewhere between the Metals on Barnhill Road and a copse at Glenageary half a mile away. With another Volunteer, I was posted on our extreme flank, guarding the entrance to the Metals, a muddy lane which skirted the local rubbish dump and marked the route of the old Atmospheric Railway along which granite was transported from Dalkey Hill to build the piers at Dun Laoghaire. It was pitch dark. After an hour of boredom, we heard whispering from further down the lane and decided that it was a courting couple, who would get the fright of their lives when we came at them with fixed bayonets and arrested them as spies. Our first indication that we were in the enemy's line of advance was when one of the lovers fired a blank cartridge into my face, turning my eyebrows to ash, and said: 'You're dead, yah bollix yah.'

We were made to lie down in the mud as befitted corpses, while a score of dim figures padded by at a crouch. The last man to pass, a blur in the darkness, paused to say, not unpityingly: 'By Jasus, yous'll be popular. They'll shoot yous at fuckin' dawn.'

As prophecy, it seemed to err on the conservative side. Theoretically, we had allowed marauding hordes to pour through our lines and inflict rape and slaughter on a slumbering Glenageary; in the realistic sense, we had, unaided, cost our unit the exercise, a silver trophy, several bets and the tatters of its self-respect. It was up to us now to report to our commanding officer that for us the war was over and our troops could stand down. Instead, we went home and to bed, leaving them, as I learned later, at their posts until dawn. No one ever came looking for me, not even to retrieve my uniform or rifle. Possibly, they balked at the risk of getting me back as well; whatever the reason, I returned the rifle by stealth, and my father wore the boots to work and, for a month afterwards, would pull up his trouser legs to look at them, saying: 'Begob, I don't know myself.'

In spite of this, I had not yet learned that as a component of any organization I had an effect comparable with that of rust on iron, for I then joined the Local Security Force as an auxiliary policeman.

This time, I came home wearing a navy-blue tunic with trousers to match, and an overcoat of a thickness which incited my mother to cry out that I was made for life. I remember only three things about the LSF: learning to operate a stirrup pump; attending our disbandment dinner, at which I up-ended a goblet of ice cream into my lap and had to stay sitting at the table all evening; and, in between, being detailed to patrol the back roads from midnight until four a.m. in the company of a man named Devaney.

A few days beforehand, I mentioned this to my friend, Liam Cooney, whose only comment was: 'If you drop a ha'penny, don't stoop to pick it up.' The remark mystified me, for I had never heard of homosexuals, let alone that Devaney was among the more indefatigable of the species: in fact, his *modus operandi* was to importune every male he encountered, on the not illogical premise that whoever buys the greater number of tickets usually wins the raffle.

We met at Dun Laoghaire police station on the appointed evening and signed the register. The duty sergeant, who knew Devaney, looked at him, then at me, then at Devaney again, long and hard. 'Mind yourself,' he said to him with great emphasis, and I recall feeling mildly aggrieved that the sergeant was solicitous for Devaney's welfare and not mine: it was, I felt, making fish of one and flesh of the other. My partner was dark and balding. His manner was that of a man who has interred his mother's corpse under the floorboards: an older generation would have called him a go-by-the-wall. To my delight, however, where films were concerned not only could he talk the hind legs off a donkey, but he had worked for a year as a technician at Ealing Studios. He had clips at home from a film called *The Ghoul*, and by the time our walk had brought us to Sallynoggin he had promised to show me these and his personally inscribed photograph of Boris Karloff. I was grinning to myself at how I would put Oliver's nose out of joint by telling him that I had met someone who had met a film star, when Devaney stopped outside the high wrought-iron gates of a large house. 'Did you hear it?' he said.

'What?'

'There's someone in there.'

We were sharing a flash lamp, and I saw its beam move like a moth through the trees and heard the crunch of Devaney's boots on the gravelled driveway. Then the light went out. 'Come here and look,' he said. I groped my way towards his voice and was hardly inside the gates when I was in a bear hug that bellowsed the air from my lungs. ''S all right, 's all right,' he muttered into my ear. His breath smelled of scallions.

He was trying to heave me against a tree. 'Get off,' I said. Whatever he was up to, it was not horseplay: I knew that much. He began to make soothing noises, and the more soothing they were the more I wanted to clout him. His arms might have been the iron hoops around a barrel: locked together, we were like one fat, staggering, four-legged man.

'Give us an oul' kiss.'

'Feck off.'

'Don't be a louser. Decent man, yes, you will. For pig iron.'

'Will you get offa me.'

I was not so much afraid of him as of finding out what it was he was after. Outrage was boiling in me; then he put his stubbled chin against my cheek. At this I gave a cry of revulsion and used the only part of me that could move, bringing my forehead down so hard on the bridge of his nose that I felt bone grate upon bone. He said 'Oh, Jay . . . *sus*', and the agonized 'sus' part of it was pure contralto. His hands flew to his face, freeing me; even so, I butted him again, this time from malice. I started walking away, and in a minute heard him skithering behind me. 'Will you wait?' he said. I walked faster, so did he, then so did I, and in no time we were at a half-trot, half-gallop, one policeman chasing another. At the corner of Adelaide Road, I heard a loud reverberating clang as if someone had struck an enormous tuning fork, and I guessed that he had run into a lamp post. He moaned in the dark, more at his own misfortune than from pain, and shouted at me: 'Run, so. Shag off. Jasus, who'd lay a finger on you? I wouldn't demean meself.' I heard him give a long wet snuffle and say: 'Bloody nerve. God, I'd want to be hard up.'

For the remainder of that long night I kept well in front of him, turning now and again to see the beam of the flashlight and keeping my ear cocked for intimations of a surprise attack. There was always the chance that a sexual optimist like Devaney might get it into his head that I had spurned him more in coyness than in anger and was coquettishly longing to play Kate to his Petruchio. He made no attempt to close the gap, however, until we were back in Dun

Laoghaire with the lighted window of the police station a lone patch of yellow in the dark street. I heard the change rattling in his pocket as he caught up with me.

'You're a terrible gobdaw,' he said, laughing. 'Did you think I was in earnest?'

I said nothing.

'I thought to meself, just for a laugh, for a bit of gas, I'll give this young fellow a fright, make him think I was one of them bum boys. Did you ever hear that expression?' He put his hand on my shoulder and took it off again as if it were scalded. 'Sure where's the harm in a joke between butties? And tell the God's truth now: you swallowed it, didn't you?'

In the lane outside the police station his voice shook like the plates on a dresser when a tram went past. 'Chancy thing to do, all the same. I mean, supposing you took it serious, like? That's how a body gets a bad name.' He cleared his throat. 'So you won't say anything, sure you won't?'

I was too tired to care. I had never in my life stayed out so late or walked so far; my knees were buckling and my bed was still another two miles away.

After the moonless night of streets and back roads the one fly-fouled ceiling light in the duty room was dazzling. When I stopped blinking I saw the sergeant straighten up from poking the turf fire and stare past me, open-mouthed at Devaney. 'Oh, holy shite,' he said. I now saw that Devaney had the makings of two black eyes. His face was daubed with dried blood from his nose, but whether his injuries were due to me or his collision with the lamp post I had no idea. 'What happened?' the sergeant asked.

'Nothing,' Devaney said, giving him a yellow smile.

'Nothing,' I said in a liar's voice.

The sergeant's head swung around at me. He had awls for eyes: you felt you could more easily hide the truth from a Redemptorist who has caught a whiff of brimstone. I knew I was going red, and of course knowing it made me go redder. The sergeant let me burn until I was the colour of the turf ash in the grate, then turned back to Devaney, and I had never seen a man look so angry. 'I told you,' he said, 'to mind yourself.'

By now, Devaney had noticed that there was blood on his fists where he had rubbed his nose while under the impression that it was running. He licked his fingers, dabbed at his face and examined the result.

'Ah, me nose,' he said. He reminded me then and there of Ronald Reagan in *King's Row* discovering that his legs had been amputated and crying out 'Where's the rest of me?'

'To mind yourself,' the sergeant said again. 'I warned you. But no, you couldn't do it. 'Twould kill you.'

'Don't aggravate me,' Devaney snarled, becoming hysterical. 'Where's there a looking glass?'

The sergeant glanced at the poker in his hand, then dropped it with a clatter as if unable to trust himself. With a violent motion he picked up the day book, a ledger three inches thick and bound in leather, slammed it shut, raised it on high with both hands and hit Devaney over the head with it. For a moment I thought his neck, chin and nose would vanish inside his chest until only the eyes were left looking out. The sergeant was normally a peace-loving man: in fact, he had the reputation of never having issued a summons or made an arrest, and he regretted the blow the instant it was struck. As Devaney looked at him in shock he put the day book back on the counter and affected to look for his page. Then, to my horror and probably the sergeant's, Devaney's face creased like silver paper and he began to cry: not silently, but with the slow, untameable siren wail of desolation. 'I want to go home,' he keened.

'Then for Christ's sakes go,' the sergeant shouted. 'Go, the pair of ye.'

As I willingly fled the room and into the lane I saw his shadow swoop upon mine on the granite wall opposite. 'And you,' he said, 'dirty elders and all as he is, you keep your gob shut about him, d'ye mind me?' The door slammed and the lamentations of Devaney became faint: I could barely hear the sergeant barking at him to give over like a decent man, to wipe his face and not go home in that state to his mother, and sure no one was saying a bloody word to him. I obeyed the injunction to keep my own counsel, not because I was afraid of the sergeant or sorry for Devaney, but because wherever the dividing line was between innocence and ignorance I was not a whit the wiser for having crossed it. I had discovered a man who liked to kiss and hug other men, and I knew that no one would ever believe me if I was foolish enough to spin such a cod of a yarn.

That period, the Emergency, was the span of my adolescence: the slow time of betrayal when two lives are led. One life, the one lived at home, the old life, is an imposture which conceals the second and is devoured by it for its trouble. For all the indecent haste to bury my childhood like a dead cat, there was an ache of loss. Whenever I saw my father coming home from work, forcing one stiff leg ahead of the other, I remembered our walks and my hand in his coat pocket and could feel again the tear in the lining and the hot bowl of his pipe. The sort he was, give him a crumb and he called it a banquet. Unlike my mother, who was forever demanding a tilly as if the whole world was her milkman, he accepted short measure as his due. When I drifted away towards the sea front and the evenings at home became fewer, he seemed either not to notice the defection or to accept it with the unconcern of a fancier releasing a pigeon that he knows will fly home. I walked in one evening to find him still up, intoning a litany of curses as he hunted for a mislaid betting slip. My lips were swollen, my chin raw, from kisses that had been as voluptuous as the collision of two boulders. The lipstick on my face looked like a nose bleed and I reeked of Agnes Doyle's perfume, one and ninepence in Woolworths and as distinctively aromatic as Jeyes Fluid, and yet all he did was look up from his foraging and say: 'Well, son, anything strange or startling?' He made it easy for me to escape, and for that reason I dawdled gratefully as one does when assured that the cell door is open.

With my mother it was different. She was a woman of passion, who let nothing and no one go from her easily. The time we moved from Kalafat Lane to St Begnet's Villas, she agreed that the sofa in the front room had become too small and infirm for me to sleep on, and it was given to Mrs Quirke next door; but no sooner had it been carried out of the house than she actually wept, already regretting the gift and moaning: 'Oh, me lovely sofa.' Now, like a woman whose lover has been attempting to steal off to greener pastures, she accepted the inevitable but was determined that if I put away childish things I would do so in the full spotlight of her anguish. She would not lift a finger to help me cut the umbilical cord. She was not my grandmother's daughter for nothing: no one else would squeeze so much juice from an injustice, real or imagined, and then devour the pith for good measure. Another woman might tear the scenery to shreds: not she. Her method of letting you know the unplumbable depths of your apostasy was to suggest – by sulking one day and simpering like a saint the next – that not a word of reproach would cross her lips. Once, it might have worked, but I knew her of an old date. Not only was she capable of pushing you away from her, towards better things, with one hand and holding you back with the other, but underneath the pain she was enjoying herself. I lied to her like a trooper. No deceit was too low, for at hand to hand combat I would not have stood a chance. She was an in-fighter who had never heard of the Marquis of Queensberry. Every Christmas, she would end the festivities with a sigh of 'Sure God only knows which of us will be alive this time twelvemonths'; but the steely look in her eye told you that however many failed to survive the year ahead, she had no intention of being one of them. If after you had quarrelled with her you held out an olive branch, she would accept it gratefully and then pare the end of it to a point, just in case the time ever came when she would need to use it as an assegai.

When I was past twenty and took the occasional drink I would have died sooner than tell her. I knew what would happen. First, she would have said: 'Sure what harm? Aren't you old enough?', with an expression on her face that threatened desolation to anyone rotten enough to begrudge me the poor pleasure of a harmless jar. That evening, to my father's stupefaction, there would be a bottle of stout poured and ready for me at tea time. My mother would fasten her eyes on me like buttonhooks while I drank it, saying more to herself than us: 'Sure stout is good for you'; and my father, wondering what the hell she was up to, would sing to her tune with: 'Oh, that's the stuff'll put the red neck on him.' But that night there would be prayers said to St Ann, and next day she would be moaning that she had a drunkard in the house and threaten to go for Father Creedon unless I took the pledge. To the day she died I still could not admit to her that I drank: the lie had gone on for too long. Shortly before I was married, my fiancée came to the house for Sunday tea, and my uncle John and aunt Chris arrived later to play Twenty-Fives. Chris, who had obviously heard of my occasional depredations, mentioned that a local pub named the Eagle House had been renovated. She gave me a sly, tight glance. 'What do you think of the improvements?' she asked.

My mother was scandalized. 'What are you talking about?' she said. 'Sure Jack wouldn't set foot inside the Eagle House?'

My fiancée stared at me. 'Why?' she asked innocently. 'What's wrong with it?'

When I was eighteen, however, drinking was something done by

133

respectable people at Christmas, and public houses were places from which you saw Joe Healy or my uncle Sonny staggering in broad daylight. My friends and I spent our money – our eightpences in the afternoons, our shillings at night time – on the pictures. We were not fans but addicts. Perhaps it was the climate that drove us indoors, for we would even sit, grumbling, through cheap second features from Monogram Studios, where the droning pre-recorded background music never matched the action. Rather than face the streets or the east wind along the sea front, we would endure the Bowery Boys and the Mr Wong series – which featured a coloured actor named Mantan Moreland who in moments of imminent disaster would roll his eyes like wagon wheels and gasp: 'Feets, do yoh stuff!' We sat sullenly through a blur of fifth-rate westerns, with rheumatoid hired guns and paunchy avengers shooting it out in the same street of the same cow-town or pursuing each other through the same dry gulch (we could identify the very rocks). We groaned when Dick Foran as a patrolman on the Lower East Side swung his eternal nightstick and polished an apple he had airily filched from a vendor's handcart; we writhed through dramas of mother love as the sheep-faced Sarah Padden wept bathetically when her son – Tom Neal or Frankie Darro – went to the bad; we sat unmoved when Johnny Downs, wearing a lettered pullover, yelled: 'Hey, kids, the Dean says we can do the show after all, and guess who's out front – Walter Ziegfelder, the big Broadway producer!'; we muttered 'Ah, for Jasus' sake' when Kay Francis nobly and lispingly renounced her youthful lover after a plea from his mother, who had said: 'Why, you're older than I am, Miss Danreuther.' We knew it was rubbish and yet we sat, our eyes glazed like zombies', living any lives in preference to our own. 'What did you think?' you would ask Liam Cooney as you both emerged from the Pavilion or the Astoria. 'A trap,' he would answer, or 'Brutal', and you agreed, knowing that you would both scrounge the pennies to see an even worse film tomorrow night.

In our picture houses there were many mansions. On Sunday evenings we queued as eagerly to see Charlie Chan, the Durango Kid and Anne Miller displaying her legs and an inch and half of bare midriff as we did to see a Fritz Lang or a Capra. We cackled when Dagwood collided with the mailman; we imitated Hugh Herbert's girlish shriek; we sneered whenever Barbara Stanwyck wept. We had only one real aversion. Being Irish, we affected to be without affectation and so detested what passed for high comedy. We called it 'codology', and it consisted archetypally of Rosalind Russell wearing a tailored suit and being mannish until Brian Aherne proved that beneath her starched blouse there existed a vibrant, desirable woman waiting to be awakened. 'Give you a pain in your arse,' Liam would mutter when Miss Russell's perennial suitor, Lee Bowman, stammered 'But, Amanda, we're engaged!' as she ran off to cook and scrub in Mr Aherne's log cabin – as big as a cathedral – in Montana. Liam had a particular liking for films that pointed a moral: not that he was more virtuous than the rest of us, but money was scarce and he never quite felt that he was getting his shilling's worth unless he was entertained *and* instructed, both at once.

Among the lads – Liam, Joe Byrne and Dan Cleary – Dan was the most remarkable. He was a walking composite of different film stars: he looked like Glenn Ford and dressed like Alan Ladd; when he flipped a coin you thought of George Raft, and he had copied his smile – wry, sleepy and dangerous – from Richard Conte. With so many cold-eyed purveyors of rough justice jostling for space inside him, it was strange that his idol was Bing Crosby: nor would you have thought so to see Dan emerging from having sat ecstatically through four showings of *Going My Way*. He would sidle out of the foyer and slip noiselessly into the shadows, his eyes flickering like lizards for signs of a lurking muscle-man from the Syndicate. He would turn up the collar of his trenchcoat, tighten the belt and, with a slow, almost mystical pass of his hand, flip down the brim of his hat. He would tap the left side of his chest to confirm that the .38 automatic was still in its holster and then, hands in pockets, move down Marine Road like a cat. To look at him, you knew he was on his way to square accounts with the hoods who had killed his best friend, even though he marred the general effect by crooning as he went:

> '... The dreams you gather will look well on you,
> Oh, I hope you're going my way, too.'

Not surprisingly, our almost daily diet of films turned us mildly schizoid. My most abiding memory is of any summer evening after the lights came up and the 'Soldier's Song' blared out, the record cracked and hissing, while we stood to attention, cigarette butts cupped in our hands, and saw with a surprise that never lessened the dinginess of the cinema: the bare walls, the upholstery dribbling from the seats, the yellow pall of smoke. Then came the crashing of iron bars, the emergency doors were flung open and daylight streamed in. We came out blinking and saw the town hall clock, the pier, the see-sawing yachts, the Killiney bus: whereas a minute previously we had been in Pago-Pago or a Park Avenue penthouse, riding shotgun across the Pecos or travelling from Oklahoma with the Joads. Walking into one world, we carried shreds of the other with us, as if we had come out of a wood with the stickybacks still clinging to our clothes.

Dan and Liam were both doing what we called steady lines. Dan's girl was Nora Kavanagh, and I can think of no better definition of true love than to tell how every year he would send her two Valentines, one signed and one anonymous – to let her think she had a secret admirer. She told Liam and Joe and showed them the card with its row of xs and a question mark for a signature. 'I dunno if I ought to tell Dan,' she would say. 'He'd be raging.' After an Irish courtship – a long one, that is, they married, went to live in Yorkshire and raised a family. I saw Dan just once across the years, a few months before he died suddenly on the brink of their silver wedding anniversary. He had aged less than any of us, possibly because he still lived in the 'forties: he smiled the same hooded smile and, his hand flapping with a languid elegance, snapped his fingers in time with a private tune.

Liam's love-life was less unruffled. During the women's yearly mission – the 'retreat', as we called it – he would wait outside St Michael's church for his girl friend to come out. There was a score or so of young men idling self-consciously outside the front gate, each one, like Liam, ashamed to be seen dancing attendance on a female who would appear after Benediction wearing the dyspeptic simper of a virgin martyr in a holy picture. One look and you knew that there would be no heavy courting for at least a week.

In those days, it was the custom for missioners to reserve their heavy artillery until the Thursday of the week, when they would launch a major offensive on impure habits and the dangers of company-keeping. This was for the benefit of domestic servants, who had Thursday evenings off and so could attend – and no one ever questioned or took exception to the implication that housemaids and mothers' helps were more likely than others to lie down, if not fall down, by the wayside. Some missioners, such as the Jesuits and Franciscans, were received apathetically, for they preached commonsense and charity respectively, and the Irish have never been noticeably partial to either. The Redemptorists were the crowd pleasers: they knocked splinters out of the pulpit and thundered forth threats of fiery damnation, making a meal of each graphic image of the torments that awaited sinners in general and sexual offenders in particular. The older members of the congregation lapped it up: they were past the age for carnal enjoyment, and it appealed to their sense of fair play to be reassured that the younger generation was not going to have its pleasures without paying the piper in the currency of sizzling flesh and jabs from white-hot tridents.

One year, when it was the turn of the Redemptorists to visit Dun Laoghaire, Liam was cooling his heels outside the church on the Thursday, waiting for his loved one to appear and give him the gist of the sermon on sex. She emerged later than usual, for it had taken the missioner the better part of an hour to describe fully the depraved nature of the average young Catholic male and to warn his flock of ewes that their rams were precisely that: crazed, lecherous beasts of the field, who would not only slake their lusts if given the least opportunity, but would commit the further and even worse sin of enjoying it. As Liam stepped forward, wet and cold from standing in a March drizzle, he expected at the very least to be fussed over for his trouble. Instead, she gave him a short, withering look of utter revulsion and went scurrying past, her head bent as if she were trying to decide between the Sisters of Mercy and the Carmelites. In time, of course, the effects of the sermon wore off, but Liam decided that he was not having 'that shaggin' carry-on' every year and found himself a new and jollier girl, named Sadie, who was a waitress and never had time off to attend the retreats.

The third member of the lads – Joe Byrne – was unattached. He attracted all the girls, except for the dedicated husband hunters, who had trained themselves to recognize a bird of passage when they saw one. He had gaiety: when rain fell on others, the sun shone on him. When he was obliged to have all his teeth pulled before he was twenty, he was in no way abashed. 'From now on,' he said, 'whenever I have a toothache I'll take them out, put them on the dresser and laugh at them.' Because Dan and Liam were courting two or three times a week, Joe and I become confederates. We patrolled the sea front, haunted the billiard hall and sat for an hour over a glass of milk apiece in the Roman Cafe; and, of course, we exchanged lewd stories and swore to the gospel truth of sexual adventures which were wholly fictitious. My mistake was to confuse Joe's charm, so freely dispensed, for intimacy, and to take seriously what to him was a game. One evening, we picked up two nurses, walked them around the town and ended up in the grounds of Monkstown Hospital where we strategically separated into pairs. Inevitably, mine was the fatter and plainer of the two: a muscular country girl; and I made the usual clumsy attempt to crown the encounter with a kiss: less because I found her desirable than because I needed proof that *I* was. She spluttered as if she had tasted vinegar.

'Arrah, g'owa that,' she said disdainfully. 'Sure smuggin' is only for childer.'

She undid the buttons of her blouse, felt for my hands and planked them upon what I felt in the dark to be the front of a torn woollen vest. 'Pull it up,' she hissed.

Fifteen minutes later, I rushed into the Roman Cafe to find Joe there ahead of me. Where losing my virginity was concerned, I was still striving among the foothills, but I could not wait to blurt out the news that I had at least reached Base Camp. 'Did you get anything?' Joe asked.

'Not half,' I said. 'She –'

'Mine was red-hot,' he said.

'She let me –'

'I got the drawers off of her,' he said. He bent towards me across the table. 'Surely to God you heard the moanin' of her? "Stop it," she says, "you're makin' me passionate." Dyin' for it, she was. I didn't leave a stitch on her, true as God.'

I listened to his recital, my feelings hovering between vicarious lust and the chastened realization that my own feat seemed puny by comparison. Joe was not one to gloss over details: he painted the picture, dot by lurid dot, of a naked female body in the throes of passion, rolling like a hoop across the hospital flowerbeds. He broke off, his eyes glazed as if remembering it.

'And what happened?' I asked. 'Did she let you?'

138

He gave me a cunning grin.

'Don't be a louser. Tell us.'

He was not to be drawn. 'Do you see the green in me eye?' he said. Then: 'Did you get a bit yourself?'

Humbly, I tendered my widow's mite. 'An old coort, that was all. She let me put me hands up her vest.'

'Is that a fact?' he said. Then his grin died as he realized that I was telling the truth. 'She let you do what?'

'I felt her chest.' It seemed even less to write home about when I said it out loud, so I apologetically added a dab of gilt to the gingerbread. 'She had a fine pair.'

'Oh, my God.' It was a groan of disgust.

'What's up?'

'You did a thing the like of that?'

For a moment I thought he was joking, that he was about to throw up his hands in mock repugnance and say what a daredevil I was or some such. Instead, he shook his head and looked at the table. 'Jesus,' he said.

'What are you carrying on about?' I said. 'You got the clothes off yours.'

His head came up suddenly. 'I did what? Easy now. You mind yourself. Do you think I'd lay me hands on a girl that way, the way you did? You say that again and I'll burst you. The Locke, that's the place for you and your sort.' The Locke was a hospital for syphilitics in Townsend Street.

I can remember the moment, but not what happened next: whether he left the table or I did. What returns, still sharp, is the realization that I had been tricked: for the first rule of a game is the acknowledgement by the players that it is one. When we regaled one another with sagas of our sexual exploits, I had in my innocence believed that Joe was speaking the truth, while I was the romancer. Now suddenly his was the head with a halo around it, and I was – and felt like – the Bully again.

I met him with Dan and Liam a few evenings later. To my surprise, he gave a whinny of delight on seeing me. 'Hey, lads,' he said, 'wait till I tell yous what the killer there did to the nurse out of Monkstown Hospital.' I could only guess that he had regretted his own moment of self-revelation as much as I had mine. At any rate, everything was the same again, and nothing was.

For three years, the sea front was our treadmill. While we waited to be set free from each other by marriage, a job, a twist of fate, a miracle, we consoled ourselves by reflecting that our exercise yard, with the railway station at one end and the public baths at the other, was for short-term prisoners. No one had ever served a life sentence: no one, that is, except Tommy Martin. Tommy pestered us. He was in his middle fifties: a thick-set, balding, unattractive man with glasses as thick as the bottoms of beer bottles. He wore a grubby tent-like raincoat and a sweat-stained hat and rode a sports bicycle with low-slung handlebars: which was extraordinary because he had only one leg. He had been shot in the ankle during the Easter Rising of 1916, and although it was a minor wound he was awarded a pension for partial disability. Unfortunately, in 1935 he was in a motor cycle accident; his leg was amputated, and as the afflicted ankle went with it his pension was stopped. The injustice rankled, and thereafter he was never quite coherent on the subject of governments. He had an artificial leg which was a poor fit: it was longer than the other by several inches, and he walked with it thrust far out to one side and had to use both hands to lift it and throw it forward. 'What he needs,' Dan said, 'is another leg to kick it with.' It seized up one day, and since Liam was of a mechanical bent Tommy gave it to him to repair. Liam took it to bits, but was either too busy or too bored to put it together again, and as the weeks passed, its owner not unnaturally became restive. One evening, we were queueing for the pictures when we saw a sight that galvanized us. It was Tommy on his bicycle bearing down on us like a Valkyrie. One empty trousers-leg flapped behind him in his slip-stream; his surviving leg was pumping up and down on the pedal; and on his shoulder a crutch was slung like a banjo. 'Hey, Cooney,' he yelled at Liam to the delirium of the queue, 'where's me whoorin' leg?'

He haunted the sea front and the Roman Cafe, trying to ease his way into conversation with groups of youths like ourselves. Like someone who carries sweets for children or lumps of sugar for horses, he always proffered his admission fee: a look at a banned magazine, perhaps, or an obscene toy bought or wheedled from a sailor off the mailboat, or a French letter which he would show us, his eyes tiny and leering behind the bottle lenses, and then carefully tuck it back inside his wallet. His only constant companion was a besotted collie named Bully. No one knew whether he inflicted himself shamelessly upon us from choice or because people of his own age shunned him. 'A dirty old degenerate,' Sean Taggart called him, 'that has nothing better to do than corrupt young lads.' Certainly he did not corrupt us, for his childish eagerness to cut a worldly figure made us feel older than he was. On first acquaintance he would treat you as an equal; then he became avuncular, dispensing unasked-for advice; finally, he was domineering, singling out one of us for criticism or ridicule. The lads had an in-bred tact and tolerance which I lacked: they would defer to him, then, when they had had enough, quietly keep out of his way. I, on the other hand, would oppose him head on; my tongue was sharper and crueller than his, and he would back off, muttering that I was too damn clever by half. I was using a sledgehammer to kill a gnat: he was harmless, and friendless apart from the dog and a girl friend: a strangely serene, demure girl whom we saw linking him into the pictures on Sunday evenings.

We heard that he was seriously ill and in St Michael's Hospital. One day, I saw him at the box office of the Picture House in George's Street, and as he took his ticket I went over. 'Are you better, then?' I asked. 'When did they let you out?'

'They didn't let me out,' he said. 'I wanted to see this fillum, so I made them give me me clothes. And as soon as I've seen it they can have me. I'll go back in and die.'

He caught hold of his artificial leg, heaved it forward and went through the swing doors into the cinema. He kept his word. He saw the film, went back into hospital and died.

As for the lads, Dan, as I have said, died suddenly of a heart attack in England. Liam married his Sadie; they reared a family of six and adopted a seventh, and they could not have been happier. Joe went to Australia, where he dropped out of sight for twenty years. Then, with the surviving members of his family convinced that he was long since dead and buried, he blithely turned up for a visit and wearing the same Cheshire Cat's grin. In fact, the only difference was that in the meantime he had found a red-headed wife and lost two fingers and his accent.

Chapter 12

They had moved to St Begnet's Villas the year before, and the new house, at the far end of the town, had an upstairs, an indoor lav, and a garden in front with an iron gate that squeaked, and now Mr Drumm came through it. Jack saw him from behind the lace curtains: he closed the gate, then gave it a look of dislike that dared it not to stay shut.

Jack knew him well to see. He lived on Dalkey Avenue in a house that had a name, Kilmore, and he was in the civil service in Dublin; a bobby's job, Jack's da called it. He was thin and stiff as a hatstand. Everything about him seemed to go downwards: his gabardine raincoat hung straight on him, his hat sat on his head without the whisper of a tilt, his umbrella could have passed for a walking stick: even the wrinkles on his face ran down from his cheekbones to his jaw. There were only two sideways things about him: his glasses with the gold rims and his lips, as thin as Lent. When a smile came on his face, it was not the kind you smiled back at: it was the kind that said what a fool he had been for having trusted someone. 'Oh, old Drumm's a queer harp,' Jack's da would say, even though Mr Drumm was ten year younger than himself.

At the rap of the brass knocker his da came up out of his chair. 'Didn't I tell you it'd be eight on the dot?' he said. ' "I'll call," says he to me, "and see the boy at eight o'clock." And is that not the time, Mag? Was I telling the truth or was I not?'

Going to the door, she gave him a look and said: 'Now you hold your tongue while he's here. Whatever's to be said to him, I'll say it, so don't you go putting in your prate.'

Once the door was open, she was as nice as pie. She made Mr Drumm sit in the good armchair by the range and told him he would have a cup of tea, in his hand, just.

'No, I will not,' he said.

'Yes, he will,' Jack's da said. 'Don't mind him. You will, you will.'

His ma already had the teapot off the range. 'You're a foolish woman,' Mr Drumm said. 'In these lean times we may take hospitality for granted.' He peeled one of his leather gloves from a hand that was red from chilblains. Jack was noticing this and the smallness of the knot in his tie when he found himself being looked at. 'Is this the boy?'

'That's Jack,' his ma said.

'John Joseph,' his da put in, not able to sit quiet if it killed him.

The spectacles caught the firelight. Mr Drumm's nose twitched: it seemed to be able to shrink back the way the horns of a snail did when you touched them. 'Your father tells me you've passed the entrance examination.'

'Yeah.'

'For a temporary clerkship.'

'Yeah.'

The grey eyes looked at him as they had looked at the front gate. 'The word you seek, my friend, is not "yeah", but "yes". I take it you have been called for interview?'

Jack felt himself go red. It was as if Mr Drumm had said: 'You may be a big fellow among your friends on the sea front, but not where I'm concerned.' He nodded, not to give the old gett the satisfaction of hearing him say 'yes'.

'Speak up. What?'

Blast him. 'Yes.'

'And they require a reference.' He turned to Jack's ma. 'I cannot see why you come to me for it. I don't know the boy.'

She put the cup of tea into his hand, flirting with him like a young one. 'Sure don't you know himself,' she said, nodding at Jack's da.

'Oh begob, he does,' his da said. 'Sure doesn't he see me at the whist drive? And who was it pruned his roses?'

'It is not my roses that are asking for a reference.' Mr Drumm tapped a drop of tea from his spoon. 'I don't recommend the civil service to anyone. I know it too well, and to my cost.' To Jack he said: 'If you take my advice you'll look elsewhere.'

'He can't pick and choose,' his ma said. 'He's six months idle since he left the Presentation.'

'Even so.'

'Sure won't it do him for the time bein',' his da said. 'Won't there be lashin's of grand jobs once the war's over?'

'Past history says otherwise,' Mr Drumm said. 'There's usually a depression.'

'Not at all.'

In Mr Drumm's voice, sleet fell. 'You're an expert, are you?'

'What are you talkin' about,' his da said, 'or do you know what you're talkin' about? Sure the Germans know the Irish are their friends, and signs on it, when the good jobs are handed out beyant in England they'll give us the first preference.'

'Who will?'

'The Jerries, amn't I tellin' you, when they win.'

His ma was holding on to the back of a chair, her knuckles white. The smile on her face looked as if it had been painted there and was flaking.

'You support the Germans, do you?' Mr Drumm asked.

There was a soft bumping noise from upstairs. Jack knew it was his mad aunt Mary rocking her pramful of dolls and banging it against the wardrobe out of temper. She had been sent upstairs so as not to make a show of them in front of Mr Drumm, and Jack remembered a story he had heard about a woman called Morty, who was like Mary, as daft as a brush. The story was that when the parish priest came to the house she was sent into the back room out of sight, with a mug of tea in her hand to keep her quiet. But in the middle of the priest's visit there was a roar out of her of 'More tea or I'll appear!' It was the 'more tea' that got her christened Morty, and Jack smiled remembering the story. 'Is something amusing you?' Mr Drumm said, hissing like a gas leak.

'No.' A woman opera singer had never let such a high note out of her.

Mr Drumm's eyes let go of him and turned back to his da. 'You're an admirer of theirs, are you?' he said. 'The Germans.'

His da laughed. 'Hitler's the man that's well able for them. He druv them into the sea in nineteen-forty and he'll do it again now. Sure what's Churchill anyway, only a yahoo, with the cigar stuck in his fat gob and a face on him like a ... a ... a boiled shite.'

'You oughtn't to mind him,' his ma said with a terrible jollity.

'I don't at all,' Mr Drumm said. He set down his cup and saucer inside the fender.

His da was only cantering before the gallop. 'Sure what luck would the English have anyway? Didn't they come into the town here and shoot decent people in their beds? But they won't see the day when they can crow it over Heil Hitler. He's the boy will give them lackery.' He tore a piece off the deaths page of the *Evening Herald* and stuck it between the bars of the range to light his pipe.

Mr Drumm was on his feet, the glove back on his hand. He spoke to Jack's ma as if there was no one in the room but himself and her. 'I can hardly testify to the boy's character on no acquaintance whatever. I have an appointment in Dun Laoghaire. Perhaps he would walk with me.'

Her face had become small. 'He will, of course. Jack, do you hear?'

'Are you off, so?' his da said. 'That was short and sweet.'

Jack went upstairs to get the brown envelope with the forms in it from the civil service. On his way back down, he heard Mr Drumm say: 'Do you mean the boy is adopted?'

He hung back on the stairs. It was like hearing an old gramophone record he had thought was in bits by now. 'And a child that was delicate,' she said. 'She tried to get rid of him.'

'Get rid?'

'Before he was born. Whatever kind of rotten poison she took. Sure Dr Enright told me, plump and plain. "Ma'am," he said, "that child will never make old bones."'

He went down the rest of the stairs and out into the garden, away from her voice and the old come-all-ye he knew by heart. At Presentation it had been bad enough; now, thanks to her, the whole of the civil service would have it. Cold needles of rain cooled his face, and after a while Mr Drumm appeared on the doorstep looking at the sky as if it had better mind itself. His ma had a hold of his arm and was saying: 'You'll do the best you can for him. You will, and God reward you'; while behind them his da gave the Nazi salute, his hand nearly knocking Mr Drumm's hat off, and said: 'We shall rise again!'

They walked down Hyde Road to Sandycove, past the Martello tower where your man, James Joyce, had lived and along by the sea wall. 'My friend,' Mr Drumm said, 'if you and I are to have dealings you will learn to speak English properly. When the Irish are not assassinating each other's character, they assassinate language instead.'

Jack nodded, too afraid of him to answer out loud.

'You speak Irish, I daresay,' Mr Drumm said.

'A bit.'

'The language of clodhoppers and fanatics. In Merrion Street I have them under me and over me: they smell of manure and have to be etherized before they'll put a collar and tie on.'

Jack looked at him for a sign that he was meant to laugh, but Mr Drumm had a face on him like mortal sin.

'You'll find out,' he said.

By the time they reached the People's Park the rain was coming down like stair-rods. Mr Drumm opened his umbrella and gave it to Jack to hold while he took a packet of Player's from his pocket and lit one without offering them. There was a sound of music keening through the rain. People came spilling from the pierhead, looking for shelter.

'There's a band on the pier,' Jack said.

Mr Drumm tilted his head back as if he was smelling the music instead of hearing it. 'The Artane Boys,' he said.

Artane was an orphanage, and Jack looked hard at him in case maybe he was making a dig, but there was no sign of it. 'Come,' Mr Drumm said, and they went up Park Road. The south-west wind brought the rain driving in at them, but Mr Drumm held the umbrella upright, as straight as himself, sooner than be dictated to by the weather. Before they had reached George's Street, Jack's trousers were sticking to his knees, and he was wondering how he would get home without the tram fare when he realized he was walking alone. He looked around and saw Mr Drumm glaring at him from the doorway of a public house.

'My friend.' He crooked a long finger.

Jack had never been inside a pub before, and a shiver went through him that was partly the pleasure of having committed a new wickedness. The lights were on and there was a smell of porter. Two men with grey paint caked dry on their hands were sitting on the wooden barstools, and beyond a partition a man in a hard hat had the *Evening Mail* spread out on the bar. 'Do you take a drink?' Mr Drumm said.

'Not yet.'

'You will, please God.'

The barman came up. "Evening, Mr D., sir. Damp old evening.'

'A bitch,' Mr Drumm said, and Jack's heart gave a jump: not at the word itself, but at the venom that contained it. 'A glass of John Jameson, and a mineral for this young man. Any kind will do: one's as pernicious as the next.'

'Still, sir, it won't harm a hair of him.'

'You heard that?' Mr Drumm said as the barman went off. '"Sir." This is one of the last outposts of civility.'

He stood at the bar like a pencil on its end. Jack climbed on a barstool. For a moment, with his feet hanging clear of the floor, he had a strange familiar feeling; then he remembered the high-chair he had sat in when he was small.

'Do you chase girls?' Mr Drumm asked.

'Pardon?'

'Female persons: do you indulge?' Steam was beginning to rise from his trousers.

Girls were not the kind of thing you talked about to old fellows that were pushing fifty or maybe past it, and still less when they were like Mr Drumm and looked as if they would eat you. Why was he so inquisitive about girls? Then Jack felt his scalp crawl at the memory of when he had gone on an LSF patrol with Sean Devaney who had chased him all over the backroads. He had asked questions, too.

'The odd time,' Jack said carefully.

'As a diversion, I don't condemn it,' Mr Drumm said. 'Chase away by all means and give them a damn good squeeze when you catch them, but be slow to marry. The maximum of loneliness with the minimum of privacy. I have two daughters myself.'

'I know them.'

'You know my daughters?' The words fell between them like hailstones.

'To see, like.'

The waiter brought the whiskey and a tumbler of water for Mr Drumm, and for Jack a lemon soda. It was nice to know that Mr Drumm was not a bum-boy after all. 'I would describe my daughters as birdlike,' he said.

If he had said that the drink in front of him was a duck egg, Jack would have agreed with him. 'Yes, I suppose –'

'Rhode Island Reds. You may laugh.'

'I wouldn't.'

'I said you may. *I* do.'

His smile was a grey hair that landed on his face, then drifted off again. He tipped water into his whiskey, watching it spread through it in yellow coils.

'The civil service is like a lobster pot, harder to get out of than into, and you seem to me not to be cut out for clerking. But if you are determined to throw your life away, who am I to hinder you? I'll write you your reference: it'll be adequate, if not glowing. I shall need to know your name.'

'Keyes,' Jack said in surprise.

'I mean your real name. You heard what your fostermother told me, didn't you? That you're illegitimate.'

Warm air touched his forehead as if a kitchen door had opened. It was like the day he had skidded and been thrown off his bicycle on Rockford Avenue, and the brake lever had gone into the back of his leg. At first there had been no pain, only the feel of the gravel under his palm and the knowledge that you could not go back in time for even those few measly seconds to undo what would happen next. It, that word, Mr Drumm's word, was the worst thing anyone had ever said to him. He thought of the scar behind his knee, still there after all these years: would he be left with a limp? his ma had asked. Through a private rain he saw the face next to him at the bar: the thin red veins of the nose, the furrows of old betrayals ploughed down the cheeks, the pale, displeased eyes.

'Don't give me that woebegone look,' Mr Drumm said. 'It's a fact. You're going to have to live with it, and you may as well make a start. Bastardy is more ignominious in a small town than a large one, but please God it may light a fire under you. Do your friends know?'

Jack shook his head. The second word, the one that began with a 'b', was even worse than the first. He wanted to go home.

Mr Drumm looked at his whiskey again, forgave it its trespasses and swallowed half of it. 'Probably they do,' he said. 'So don't tell them: they won't thank you for spiking their guns. What ails you? Now look here, my friend: tears will get no sympathy from me. I say, we'll have done with it. People will take me for a pederast. Your nose is running: wipe it.'

'I haven't a handkerchief.'

'Well, either go the lavatory or drink your lemonade.'

'It's lemon soda.'

'Don't be impudent.'

Jack wiped at his face with his sleeve, gave Mr Drumm as dirty and scarifying a look as he could manage and took a gulp of the lemon soda, realizing a second too late that he should have told the old gett to stick it.

He had never wanted to go into the civil service: it was his uncle John's and his aunt Chris's idea. They had bullyragged him. 'Sure, Mag,' Chris had said to his ma in that voice of hers that walked on tiptoe for fear it might step in something, 'he'll be secure for life and he'll have a pension. Finished for the day at a quarter past five and one o'clock on Saturdays, and there won't be a house in the country he need be ashamed to walk into. How bad he'll be! Look where John is today.' Jack had looked, and saw his uncle John in his felt tartan slippers, in the middle of the shining furniture that smelled of wax, his pink, plump fingers clasped across his watch-chain. Behind him on the sideboard was the wedding picture of himself and Chris, with holiday snaps from Greystones huddling under it like fry under a mackerel. 'Oh, the regular hours, yes, just so,' John said. 'And he'll receive increments.'

'By me soul, he will, and I'll see to it,' his ma had said, getting muddled and thinking he meant sacraments. She had looked at Jack, seeing him in a collar and tie for life.

'You're a sulker, aren't you?' Mr Drumm said. He beckoned to the barman. 'Now listen to me. As a government clerk, you will not go by your foster-parents' name but by your own. Like it or not, that is the position. So you will tell me what that name is and have done with this nonsense. Well?'

'Byrne.' He mumbled it.

'John Byrne.' Mr Drumm held it under his nose and sniffed at it. 'As common a name in Dublin as John Smith is in London. Someone seems to have lacked imagination. Or can't have been bothered.'

The barman brought him another whiskey. Jack looked to see if the two men with paint on their hands were listening. One of them was saying: 'Fuckin' little whoor the like of him, offerin' to crease me. Little fuckin' head-the-ball that couldn't pull the skin off a fuckin' rice puddin', even if his fuckin' oul' wan helped him.'

'Perhaps you would rather change places with them,' Mr Drumm said, meaning the two men. 'Their birth certificates are probably unblemished, and yet what have they to show for it? Like the old man, your foster-father. There are millions like him: inoffensive, stupid and not a damn bit of good. They've never said no in their lives or to their lives, and they'd cheerfully see the rest of us buried. They deride whatever is beyond them with a laugh, a platitude and a spit. From people too ignorant to feel pain may the good Lord deliver us.'

'Sure he's on'y a bollix and always will be a bollix,' the other man was saying to comfort his friend.

The hair appeared across Mr Drumm's face again. 'Even so, I have a fondness for him. He does an honest day's work, and if a fool of a woman reneges on him at a whist drive, well, she won't do it a second time. Yes, he's colourful. But then the dangerous ones are those who amuse us.'

Whether his da was being blackguarded or praised was as broad as it was long: he was no match for Mr Drumm, whose tongue could twist and cut like a fretsaw. From the beginning, he had felt that every answer he gave, or whether he smiled or was solemn, was being stored in Mr Drumm's purse of a mind: he was being put through an exam, but without even knowing what the questions were. A tram went past outside: over the stained glass of the window he saw its lights stuttering past. Its wheels made the rain hiss in the tracks. He searched his brain for, and found, an excuse to go. He said: 'Is your friend meeting you here?'

'I drink in this establishment,' Mr Drumm said, 'because in Dalkey every cornerboy knows your business.' He frowned. 'My friend? What friend?'

Jack slid down from the barstool. 'You said you had an appointment.'

There was a kind of glass bubble attached to the upside-down Jameson bottle behind the bar. It was filled with whiskey, and Jack had twice watched the barman touch it with the rim of a glass, at which it would empty and then, as if in a conjuring trick, fill up again. Now Mr Drumm's face emptied in the same way. 'So I did,' he said in a voice like a knife. Before Jack could wonder what ailed him, he drew a long slow breath through his nose as if that was how he filled his face again, and the new look that came on it might have been of a man who had been snapped at by a dog he had stopped to pet.

'I see you're anxious to be off,' he said. 'I won't bore you any further.'

The change in him was so sudden that Jack stood dumb. All he had done was to be polite, and now Mr Drumm's eyes were blistering him with their disgust. He thought to say that he had promised to meet a fellow down the town, but as he made to speak Mr Drumm cut him short.

'It's unlikely that we shall meet again. Good evening to you.'

To prevent an answer, he turned away quickly, back to his one true friend, golden in the glass. It was not until Jack was half-way home, the rain playing melodeon music in his shoes, that a thought brought him to a standstill. It was the realization that Mr Drumm had had no appointment this evening, except with him.

A month later, when Jack was called for his interview, his da said: 'Oh, old Drumm must have gev you a toppin' reference. Sure didn't I tell you he would?' That evening he shaved, put on a collar and tie, shined his good boots and called upon the lady who lived in Greylands, a big house behind the railway. He told her how she wouldn't know a bit of that back meadow of hers if only the stones and stumps of trees were cleared to hell out of it, and offered to come and do the work every evening when he was finished at Jacob's. When the lady asked about money, he gave a wave of his hand as if he was a millionaire doing it for a hobby. 'Whatever you say yourself, ma'am,' he said, and off he trotted.

'How much is she paying you?' his ma asked.

'She won't see us stuck,' his da said.

'How much?' she asked.

He sat down to unlace his boots. 'Do you know,' he said, 'I have a corn on me that's a bugger.'

In his whole life he had thought bad of demanding his due. Now, he made a great show of rubbing his foot, taking care not to look at her until at last she turned to the sprig of blessed palm that was pinned to the door and asked it if it saw what she had to put up with. For all that, and with the extra money certain – and even if it was a hundred pounds she would never give him the satisfaction of hearing her say that it was enough – she put down five shillings deposit on a suit for Jack and bought him a new shirt in McCullagh's. 'Sure you can't let him go mixin' with high-up people,' his da said, 'and the arse out of his trousers.'

'That will do you with your language,' she said.

'Oh, be the hokey, aye,' he said. 'If he wants to work with old Drumm he'll have to smarten himself.'

It was no good telling him that the civil service was spread over the length of Dublin and with tens of thousands of people in it: his da had it stuck inside his head that you could fit the whole shebang inside Mammy O'Reilly's shop in the town. Even so, the mention of Mr Drumm's name, never mind the thought of ever seeing him again was enough to make Jack's heart lurch like a sick dog.

His da was paid three pounds for the two weeks it took him to clear and mow and make a meadow of what had been a field. He came home one evening, and his tiredness and the scythe carried over his shoulder made him look like the old year going out. 'I don't need a suit,' Jack suddenly shouted at him. 'Spend it on yourself.'

'And what the hell would I do with it?' his da said. 'Isn't herself and me grand, wantin' nothin' from no one?' He laughed. 'Oh, a comical boy. Sure certainly you need a suit.'

'Doesn't know when he's well off,' his ma said. 'Oh, the more you do for them ...'

'You needn't buy it,' he said, 'because I won't wear it.'

So the suit was bought, the sleeves taken in and the legs let out, and off he went in it for his interview. They asked him what 'DV' meant and if he had read *The Collegians* and knew what play was taken from it and what opera; and from there he was sent to a room high up in the GPO, where a doctor with the face and voice of a Scotch terrier banged on his chest and barked: 'Frightful lot of TB around ... the whole damn country is riddled with it.' Jack felt his legs go weak, and he was seeing himself wasting away in Peamount Sanatorium when the doctor said: 'All clear. You'll eat a few more Christmas dinners.' The following Friday, he walked into a waiting room that was as full of new suits as his own, and was given forms to sign, including one that threatened desolation if he opened his mouth about whatever work he did. One of the other lads was shunted off to Industry and Commerce and another two to Defence, beyond in Glasnevin, and when it was Jack's turn he was told to report to the Land Commission. He was relieved to know that at least he would not have to trudge across the city every day to the North Side, and he wondered if maybe he would be working close to his uncle John.

He walked up Merrion Street to Number 24 and climbed stairs and went through corridors like rabbit warrens until he reached a room where the sunlight hammered unheard against the dirt on the windows. A man with a reddish moustache and policeman's eyes looked at the form Jack handed him and swept it to one side with the back of his hand. 'Cork Collection,' he said. As Jack waited, feeling as thick as he was meant to, he picked up the *Irish Press*, flung it open so that the pages snapped, and said from behind it: 'See the Higher Staff Officer, Cork Collection Branch.' Closing the door, Jack heard someone in the room laugh and say: 'That's it, Tom . . . show them who's boss.' He went back down the stairs, along a narrow yard where bicycles stood in their racks like old men on crutches, and into an ugly concrete building that was called Collection Branch. On the third floor he found a long room with maybe thirty people in it, and to his amazement half of them seemed to be beggarmen. Nearly all the men wore jackets that were mouldy with age: the pockets and seams were torn, the lapels had peeled like wallpaper in a slum, the padding foamed from the shoulders. If there had been mugs of cocoa on the desks instead of papers and dockets it might have been that the St Vincent de Paul were giving a social. He was to find out later that this was how they dressed for work, that they hung up their outdoor jackets along with their lives on the racks at the end of the room.

He said to the nearest person, a blonde girl wearing a blue overall: 'I'm to see the Higher Staff Officer.' She went red, like a nun breaking her vows, and whispered: 'The end table.'

That was another thing he had to learn: that what you sat at was not a desk but a table. He went down the room, marching in time to the squeak of his shoes. Not a head was raised as he walked by, but the eyes glinted at him and went dull again like half-buried bits of broken glass. At the end of the room a man sat at a table that was placed at right angles to the others to mark his apartness. His fingers rested on its edge: he was looking at a single sheet of paper the way a pianist might look at music before playing it. He sat stiff and unmoving. After a time, his eyes came up slowly. He sniffed.

'Yes?'

Jack said: 'They told me I'm to work here.'

'I suppose,' Mr Drumm said, 'there have been greater co-incidences.'

He was put to work writing what were called Receivable Orders. These were dockets which farmers sent in with their half-year's rent: you copied down the name and address, the serial number and the name of the townland: you folded the docket and put it into a brown envelope so that the address showed in the window, and by a quarter past five the envelopes stood around you in wobbling towers. On the first day, he went at lunchtime to Bewley's in Grafton Street; the noise, the smell of food and the waitresses darting past him made him feel like an interloper, and he came out again. He bought a cream bun and two potato pancakes in Merrion Row and ate them between there and the office. When he came in Mr Drumm beckoned to him.

'My friend.'

'Yes, sir.'

'The required form of address here is not "sir", but "mister". Did you eat lunch?'

'Yes, Mr Drumm.'

'If you did, it must have been perfunctory.'

He did not know what the word meant or how to answer. Just then a woman with a red bony nose came in from the landing and laid a file on Mr Drumm's table. She snuffled and said: 'I was tode to gib you dis for addention.' He did not answer, but looked at her as if she had flowed in under the door in a pool. She backed away, said 'Dangs very mudge' and went.

Mr Drumm's fingers tangoed on the table. 'Mr Byrne,' he said, 'or if you prefer, Mr Keyes Byrne – which seems to me to be not only an attractively uncommon name but an acceptable compromise – I do not know whether I have a by now long forgotten reason for disliking that woman or whether I have a natural prejudice against any female person with a perpetual drop dangling from the end of her nose, but may the curse of the Seven Snotty Orphans of Kilmacanogue alight upon her, and that, Mr Keyes Byrne, is a particularly virulent curse.'

Jack made himself smile, not only because he was expected to, but to show Mr Drumm that he knew he had been forgiven for the evening in the pub. The truth was, it made no differ: not now. He sat at his table, and the thought filled him like lead that he would climb the same stairs for ever to sit and write Receivable Orders like the one in front of him: to James Ahearne, Butteen, Gortnaroe,

Buttevant, Co. Cork. The bare top branches of a tree outside the window told him with a jeer that he would be there to see the leaves appear and grow, then turn and fall, then grow again. At his back there were high cupboards packed tight with bundles of files that were tied up with coarse twine and bulged out through the doors like a murderer's leavings. There were coloured postcards from Glengarriff and Lourdes pinned to a black screen behind the typist's chair. The walls of the room were green until half-way up, then what had been cream five years ago; and from the windows you could see the backs of the tall Georgian houses that lined Merrion Street like oul' ones who were the height of fashion from the front and in flitters from behind. A man with a walk that longed to be a trot came into the room and swapped his tweed jacket for one so shiny you could shave in it. 'Ho-ho,' he said, 'making a show of us!' meaning that Jack had come back too early from his lunch. The afternoon became a snail that crept towards a quarter past five. At four o'clock, a girl put a mug of tea and a Marietta biscuit in front of Jack. 'It's a penny a day for the tea,' she said, 'and a ha'penny for the biscuit. I'll collect from you on pay day, and will you bring in your own cup?'

He swallowed hard to force the tea past the the lump in his throat and watched the biscuit crumbs fall like snow on the knees of the new trousers he had worn, eejit that he was, to go into prison. All he could think of was escaping: soon, somehow. One morning when he was small, his da and ma had told him they were taking him to the pictures: a special film, they said; but the tram went past the Picture House. He saw the iron gates pulled across where you paid to get in, and knew he had been tricked. They took him to Loughlinstown Hospital, where he was kept for a week and given Black Jack to drink, and all thanks to Dr Enright who thought his sore throat was diphtheria. Now he had been fooled again, but by himself. He had listened to his ma talking a hole in a pot about the pension and the three pounds fourteen a week and to his aunt Chris with her Quality accent and her airs and codology, and had given in to them because Yes was always easier to say than No.

He looked at the man at the next table, a Mr Kennedy, with a bald head and a fat mad moon of a face, and told himself it was not too late: he would not end up here and half dead like the rest of them: the world was outside, he would still get back to it. A voice at the edge of his mind asked: how? It told him he had no trade, that he knew bugger all except for his films and what his ma called his curse-o'-God books, so where did he think he was off to? An old Dublin cat-call came into his head: Where are you goin' with no bell on your bike? On the train home to Dalkey he sat, not able to open his *Picturegoer* for the *Evening Herald* on his left and the *Evening Mail* on his right, and let his thoughts drift like a boat among islands. At Sandymount Halt he was taking a correspondence course; by Booterstown he was writing a book that would make a mint; between Seapoint and Salthill he had met a girl with her da a millionaire; and by the time the train was slowing down between the green banks after Glenageary his future was as golden and indistinct as a city in the evening, caught between him and the sun.

As the weeks went by, the faces around him in the office began to lose their sameness and have names. There was Mickey Bracken at the head of the room: a little red-faced man who was the best and friendliest company in the world until you were out of sight and earshot, and by the time he had stopped blackguarding you it was not a character you had, but confetti. There was Mr Hozier, a hunchback, who ran like a spider. In the office, he was a crawler who would inform on you for not dotting an 'i'; outside it, he would keelhaul you into the nearest pub as if it was your birthday and his own. 'Oh, Frankie,' his sister would sob as he rushed past her into the house, ossified drunk and only coming home to get enough money to make a night of it, 'what would Mammy say, RIP, if she could see the state of you.' 'Ah, bollix,' Mr Hozier would say with great jollity, giving a laugh that came up from hell, and go scuttling out to be the toast of Searson's until closing time and of Dolly Fawcett's after.

There was Caroline Kennelly, who had hair like wire wool dyed red, when you could see it through the cigarette smoke. Every so often, she would send off a splinter of glass to Player's or Carrera's or Carroll's, pretending she had found it in one of their cigarettes, and back would come a free tin of two hundred with a letter begging her forgiveness. It was not dishonest, she said, because she spent the money she saved on holidays in youth hostels, and there was no pastime more wholesome. Then there was Johnno Fox, who told Jack he was doing a red-hot line with one of the Moonbeams out of the Queen's Theatre. 'She's bloody massive,' he said. 'Built like the

Brick Wall of China.' One evening, he called to the Moonbeam's house with a bag of buns and oranges, only to find that her husband, a ship's stoker, was home from sea, and he shagged Johnno into the street, and the buns and oranges after him.

And there was Mr Kennedy, who sat nearest to Jack. He had been shell-shocked in the First World War and was fat and bald, with amazed blue eyes. He played the organ in the Protestant church in Ranelagh and was nicknamed 'Silent' Kennedy. He would sit for half the day with his pink, plump hands in his lap like two dead piglets, and not a word out of him until, with a shout that made you jump, he would say: 'I weighed meself this morning in the men's lavatory in Ballsbridge'; and that was his conversation for the day. If you had sense, you did not trick-act with him. He was staring into a charge book one day when a country-faced, tight-bummed woman from the Hollerith section tried to take it for herself. 'Easy, easy, easy,' he said, not letting go, and there was a tug-o'-war between them, with Mr Drumm looking on like a waxwork. The woman won. She snatched the charge book away from him, gave a crow of triumph into his face and turned her back on him; at which Mr Kennedy gave her such a kick up the behind that if there had been a hurdle in front of her she would have cleared it.

Every morning when you came in, you signed the attendance book, and Mr Drumm would carry it off to his own table to mark the names of the latecomers in red ink. One day, he made to pick up the book, then looked closely at it. 'Come here and sign your name, Mr Kennedy,' he said.

'Oh, I signed me name,' Mr Kennedy said without budging from his chair, and sure enough Jack had seen him bending over the book with a pencil in his hand.

'You did not sign your name,' Mr Drumm said. 'You will come here and do so now.'

'Oh, I signed it right enough,' Mr Kennedy said happily.

A redness was spreading into Mr Drumm's face. 'And I tell you you did not. Now sign this book or be marked absent.'

Mr Kennedy just grinned as if he was too cute to fall for an old trick the like of that. Mr Drumm's finger stabbed at the book like the needle of a sewing machine. His voice was hoarse with rage.

'Do as I say!'

There was a hush in the room as Mr Kennedy got up from his

table, taking with him the magnifying glass he used for reading. He was bent over the book for a long time, and when he straightened up his face threw a pink, happy light on Mr Drumm.

'Ah,' he said, 'did you rub it out on me?'

At first, Jack had thought that the people around him were mummies that needed burying, but before long he realized that he was in an orchestra of head cases, with Mr Drumm as the conductor. He could never be as unhappy again as he had been on that first day, but more than ever he longed to be free of the place. He had been there for six months when a man named Paddy Malone remarked to him: 'A great ending to a great play.'

'What is?'

'That tune you were whistling: "Keep the Home Fires Burning". It comes in at the end of *The Plough and the Stars*. You know: by O'Casey.'

He shook his head.

'You what? You call yourself a Dublinman and you never heard tell of O'Casey?'

'Well, yeah, I *heard* of him, but –'

'Lord God, I'm from Cork where they eat their young, yet I know him backwards. And you the fellow with his nose forever stuck in a book. What are you reading there, anyway?' He picked up a book from Jack's table. '*The Garden* by L. A. G. Strong.' He grunted. He had fair hair, turning iron grey. His mouth was set in a pretended disgust. 'Are you having me on or what? You never heard of *The Plough and the Stars*?'

'No.'

'And you're the man who wants to write books?'

Someone had been spreading yarns. 'I never said I –'

'Listen to me. It's on at the Abbey, so would you ever go down there and see it and not be making a holy show of yourself.'

He winked and strolled away, singing 'Keep the Home Fires Burning' in a Cork tenor that made Mr Drumm's eyes swing around like searchlights.

That evening, Jack went to the Abbey Theatre. He had never seen a play before, except for *The Colleen Bawn* on Dalkey town hall, where the girl was thrown off the rock into the lakes of Killarney, and all the hard chaws had stood up to see her land on a mattress. Now, he saw an actor named McCormick, who was as real as Mr

Quirk in Kalafat Lane had been, or Jack's uncle Sonny, or any of the old lads who stood spitting at Gilbey's corner or the harbour wall: a foxy-faced jackeen in a hard hat, who would look to gut you one minute and be a decent skin the next. And there was a younger actor named Cusack who was the Young Covey, and when he changed out of his working clothes and remembered to take the packet of Woodbines from his overall pocket, the people nudged one another and whispered: 'Oh, that's very good.' But it was more than the acting that made Jack stand outside the theatre afterwards, looking towards the roof tops for the red glow of Dublin burning that he had seen through the window of Bessie Burgess's attic room. The life that roared through the play itself had spilled over from the stage, sweeping him with it so that he knew he would never again be content just to sit and watch and applaud with the rest of them. The thought burned him like fever.

He went along Marlborough Street to the quays, and from the dark of the river the east wind leaped at him like a robber. He held his coat collar shut, and his hand shook with cold. He went trotting past the row of hansom cabs and the snorting horses, racing the lights of the last train as it crossed the loop line bridge to Tara Street. The guard held the door of the last compartment open for him, and he sat down opposite a young man and a girl. The man looked sulkily at him: by interloping Jack had spoiled his chance of a coort.

The pair of them could strip to their skins for all he cared. He looked away from them through the window and saw his reflection in the dark glass. It was amazing how calm he looked. His breath in the unheated compartment threw a mist upon the glass, but even then he could see, as if it was out there by the tracks, the door he would escape through.

Chapter 13

My father lived to be eighty-three, and in retrospect I am surprised that he managed it. Once, while I was walking home from the railway station, a friend of mine roared past me on his motor cycle, goggled and gauntleted and taking Gilbey's corner at an angle that was an insult to centrifugal force, and to my horror I saw that my father, then past seventy, was on the pillion. His pipe was clenched between his teeth, he was holding his walking stick with one hand and keeping his hat on with the other, and unless there were choirs of angels holding him in place there seemed no reason why he should not go hurtling through any one of Dalkey's four score of shop windows. I walked the rest of the way home on legs of indiarubber, afraid to turn the next corner and see a crowd around what was left of him and muttering that he had been a great character and sure hadn't it been a shocking winter for deaths. Instead, I found him in his armchair next to the range, banging his pipe on the bars and saying: 'Was that yourself I passed in the town, son? Michael Keogh gev me a lift on his motor bike, so I cem home in great style.' He rubbed his knees. 'The oul' legs has me buggered.'

In old age he was troubled by rheumatics and increasing deafness. Because of the first, he insisted on always walking in the middle of the road, claiming that his legs were too stiff for stepping on and off pavements. Because of the second, he failed to hear a motor scooter bearing down on him from behind, the rider a youth of such sensitivity that his reaction to the sight of an elderly man stomping along directly in front of him was to cover his eyes. I was newly married at the time, and when my wife and I called to pay our Saturday visit we were met on the doorstep by my mother, her eyes dark and frightened and yet a-glint with the satisfaction of one who has been prophesying death and desolation for years and not a word of thanks for it. She told us that my father had been run over and was in St Michael's Hospital asking for me; then, with her news given and her moment past, her face went small and widowed, and she walked into the kitchen as if practising to be alone in it from this day out. I ran to the bus stop, faltering to a walk at the thought of the ordeal ahead and half-hoping, to my shame, that the worst would be over by the time I arrived. Half an hour later, I walked into a ward where my father was sitting up, scrubbed pink and looking at the list of runners in the *Irish Press*. Before I had time to say a word, I discovered why he had so urgently asked to see me. When he had been knocked down he had cut open the palm of his left hand, over which there was now a wad of cotton wool criss-crossed with surgical tape. He nodded towards his penknife and a plug of Yachtsman's on the bedside locker.

'Amn't I nicely handicapped?' he said. 'Would you cut that up for me, there's a good boy. Do you know, I'm gummin' for a smoke.'

If the old times – his times, that is – could be said to have ended at a particular moment, it was probably in 1948 on the night of the last tram. I went to stand with him among the crowd at the bakery corner at midnight and waited to hear its iron shout and see it light up the lace curtains of Ulverton Road as it crawled towards the breakers' yard or, what was worse, to have its carcass survive, like a beached leviathan's, as a greenhouse in a back garden. Good riddance, we thought: tomorrow we would have double-decker buses, sleek as a new haircut and blustering with power as they rushed us to Nelson's Pillar in thirty-five minutes instead of the trams' forty-five. The tramcars were dinosaurs, and we did not know then how much we would miss them. They sang. On a bend, the wheels would croon in the tracks, while overhead the trolley hummed in tune; and the bell clanged as much in celebration as warning. The older models were open on the top deck at the front and rear: you walked the length of the tram to the front, hands in pockets to show off your sea legs, pitting your weight against the sway; you sat, lording it over the groundlings – the walkers and the cyclists, shivering along the cobblestones – and felt the wind go tearing past as you hung on for the double bend and the dip and plunge into the main street of Glasthule, then heard the tenor of the wheels deepen and draw breath as you surged upwards, breasting the hill that was like a sea wave into the beginnings of Dun Laoghaire. We did not travel by tram: we voyaged.

That night, the last tram was not allowed to die with dignity: the crowd on board and the others that surrounded it took for souvenirs whatever could be torn away. The destination roll fluttered from the top deck; before it was caught hold of and pulled to pieces you could read the names: Rathmines, Harold's Cross, Dartry, Fairview, Dalkey, Phibsborough, Donnybrook, Inchicore, Ringsend. A pane of glass broke, the crowds grew rougher, and I heard my father say: 'Aisy, go aisy, who are you shovin'?' We went back home, taking the short cut across the waste ground by the Green Bank, the sparks flying from his pipe in the pitch dark, and he said: 'Oh begob, aye, the buses will be a great improvement. We won't know ourselves.'

That was, I think, the last time we went anywhere together, just he and I, but the last tram sticks in my mind for another reason. It was as if there was a winter wind blowing bits of his life away, and he watched them go cheerfully with no more comment than 'That's a ha'sh oul' wind startin' up.' There were his cronies, already gone or soon to go: Oats Nolan, Gunger Hammond and the rest. There were the Jacobs and their like: the Quality: sidling away and leaving the field, and the croquet lawn, to the runners-in: the gombeen men and their wives with backsides that sang of soda bread and spuds; advertising men called Brendan or Dermot, puff adders who wore blazers with braided crests that were Gordian knots and served gin and tonic by the tennis court in tumblers like baby ice floes; builders and tearers-down, huxters and chancers, the jumped up and the dragged up. They were in charge now, and while my father had barely the schooling to write out a betting slip, he recognized, when he saw it, a ring from a Hallow-e'en barm brack masquerading as a gold one. The Jacobs had looked upon him as a breed apart, a separate species: he was a servant, to be looked after and left alone, as incapable of deceiving them as was the scythe he used to fell the meadowgrass; to the newcomers he was one of themselves and, as such, a reminder to them of how far they had climbed in the world, and to him of how far he had not. Knowing their own capacity for slyness, they stood over him as he worked and watched him when he left for the day in case he might be taking home pears from the orchard or tomatoes from the greenhouse. What was more, instead of calling him 'Keyes' as the Jacobs had done, they called him '*Mr* Keyes', and that was the measure of their ignorance; for God's sake, he would tell you, the old shawlies walking the roads called him 'Mr'. Whenever my mother hearkened back to the Jacobs and the meanness of the pension of ten shillings a week, he would for once stand up to her.

'What are you talking about,' he would say, 'or do you know what you're talking about? Hadn't they style to them? Weren't they Quality? And what are the ones that are in it now? Whoors' ghosts, that's what!'

It was not only the Jacobs and his comrades that were being swept away like rags in the wind. The trams, the Wicklow regatta every August bank holiday, the Sunday afternoons at the Picture House, fishing for conger off the rocks in Dillon's Park, the open fields at Castlepark where he walked the black dog – council houses stood there now: all were as dead and gone as was our next-door neighbour, Mr Quirk, whose hard hat would scrape our lintel as he loomed in, wiping his moustache to leave room on it for the froth of his Christmas morning bottle of stout. And while my father's world was being pared away, I was trying to find one of my own.

Luckily for my sanity, I had no way of knowing that I was to be in the Land Commission for fourteen years. God tempers the wind to the shorn lamb, and I survived from one week to the next by convincing myself that deliverance was, magically, just at hand. I detested the place so much that I refused to sit for the examination in Irish which, once passed, would have meant a rise in pay and eligibility for promotion: I was afraid that the extra money might have corrupted me in my resolve to be quit of the place. My time there was not a complete waste: I made a few friends, joined the dramatic society and began to write plays, but the work would not have taxed the brain power of a simpleton, and there was never an afternoon when I did not walk out into Merrion Street without feeling like a prisoner on bail.

For eleven of my fourteen years there, wherever I looked I saw the thin, affronted shadow of my superior, Mr Drumm. I have always known that when people come too close to me too soon, the relationship is destined to end bitterly. In Mr Drumm's case, my fear of him made a falling out all the more inevitable: trying not to offend him was like crossing a minefield on crutches. The words 'like' and 'dislike' were not a currency employed by him: he either approved or he disapproved. With hindsight, I realized that he toyed with the idea of moulding me into a kind of surrogate son – the fact that I was adopted may have encouraged him to believe that it was open season on strays – but of course I proved a disappointment. Everyone did, in time. He watched you for signs of frailty, and his scrutiny unnerved you until at last you faltered, stumbled, fell and were banished from his good opinion. He was as volatile as nitro-glycerine. Once, when he returned from two weeks' holiday, I asked: 'Did you have a nice time, Mr Drumm?' He looked at me as if I were selling raffle tickets and replied with one word: a cold, crushing 'No' that closed the subject like a vault door.

In his moments of good humour he became skittish. Once, he met me in O'Neill's of Merrion Row, and before I could finish one drink he had ordered the next. When I protested that I had had enough, he said: 'You are too cunning by half, my friend. You refuse to let yourself be known, and I intend to draw you out.' If he meant to get me drunk, he was unsuccessful: my terror of him was such that if he had poured an iron lung of stout down my throat I would not have slurred one syllable. An hour later, we were standing, he and I, on the platform of Westland Row station when through the barrier came two redhaired, saucer-eyed girls.

'Mr Keyes-Byrne,' he said, his voice no less like splinters of broken glass in spite of eight John Jamesons, 'the young women approaching us are my daughters. They have been to see *The Yeomen of the Guard* at the Gaiety Theatre. If you say one word to them of where we have been tonight or what we have been doing, I shall kick the balls out of you in the morning.'

The Irish love failure: in their folklore success is inexcusable, but the fumbled ball, the lost promotion, the one drink too many are to them the stuff of romance: they turn the winner's laurels into a salad for the loser to eat, adding clichés for seasoning. And so, in the office, it was an article of faith that Mr Drumm had a brilliant mind and could have become Principal Officer, or even Chief Clerk, but for his venomous tongue. Whatever about his unsung talents, I knew that he had called the Establishment Officer 'a rogue and a blackguard' to his face. His contempt was withering and unafraid. He had no real wit, but where others spluttered or mumbled he aimed for the throat, his voice charged with loathing, the invective almost aphoristic in its phrasing. Our Assistant Principal, whose powers of riposte were feeble enough without being further handicapped by a speech impediment, would quake with dread when Mr Drumm's face, red-veined and furious, appeared in his doorway; and within minutes every epithet would be travelling by way of bush telegraph from Accounts Branch in Merrion Square to the Congested Districts Board in Hume Street.

In our room on the top floor of Collection Branch, Mr Drumm brooked no meddling from outside: none of us would fall into the fire of another's wrath while he was there to keep us sizzling in his own frying pan. He was a religious man, who went to Mass daily during Lent – I think, to warn God to pull His socks up – and thought of himself as a benevolent despot. In this role, he would permit a group of us to play penny poker quite openly on Christmas Eve, but anyone who left off wearing a necktie in high summer would be told: 'This is not a factory!' The quietest person in the office was a young, bespectacled fellow named Lynch, who never gossiped and rarely spoke: probably because of his partial deafness. One afternoon, he walked down the room to Mr Drumm and asked for the attendance book.

'For the what?'

'It's five o'clock,' Lynch said. 'I want to sign off.'

Mr Drumm raised his nose and took aim at him along the length of it. 'I,' he said, 'will tell you when it is five o'clock. Go back to your place.'

Lynch cupped a hand to his ear and said: 'What?'

Mr Drumm put his hands around his mouth like a megaphone and yelled: 'I said, sit ... down!'

To our astonishment, Lynch simply walked to the door, slammed it behind him and was gone. The only sound in the room was the muffled funeral drums of fingers beating on the surface of the end table. I had set myself the task at the time of memorizing all of *The Rubaiiyat of Omar Khayyam*, and a particular stanza came into my head:

> What, without asking, hither hurried whence,
> And, without asking, whither hurried hence?
> Another and another cup to drown
> The memory of this impertinence!

On the following morning Lynch came in, placed a sheet of paper on Mr Drumm's as yet unoccupied table, then sat at his own place, opened the *Irish Times* as usual and proceeded to read Myles na Gopaleen's column. The rest of us were eaten by curiosity to know the abjectness of what we assumed was his note of apology, so while Arthur Nolan kept watch for Mr Drumm on the stairs I sneaked a look at what Lynch had written. It consisted of a single sentence:

Mr Drumm: My time is five o'clock, which is subject neither to the idiosyncrasies of your watch nor the vagaries of your temperament.

S.O. Loinsigh, Clerical Officer

To Mr Drumm's ears, abuse from above was a battle-cry; impudence from below was different, and by that afternoon Lynch had quietly faded from our midst to another room in another branch, and, shortly thereafter, from the civil service.

Mr Drumm made of me a confidant. We travelled into town by the same train, and during the journey he would hold forth upon such subjects as the congenital foolishness of women ('A cacophonous gaggle'), pederasty ('That man Kelly is a known pervert. Shun him!') and a fellow staff officer named Mr Crean ('He spits on me as he speaks. I move away from him, and he follows me and spits on me again'). He gave me advice on becoming a writer: 'Never describe an experience until it is long past. Assimilate it as you would food. Let it turn into calcium and protein, with the waste matter excreted.' This reminded him to take his indigestion tablets. He turned a belch into a small gasp and said: 'The mind has bowels, too, you know.'

We fell out, of course; or, rather, he did with me. I never found out why: perhaps I betrayed a confidence, or he may have seen a smile or heard a laugh which he took for mockery. One wet morning, I took shelter with him by the bookstall on the platform of Dalkey station and said something inane like 'That's a damp one.' He did not look at me. He said 'Obviously!' as if the word were a foul taste, opened his umbrella and went out to stand in the rain. That was the end of his experiment in parenthood. For some weeks afterwards, he caught an earlier train, not to avoid me but to arrive at the office before I did and mark me late. He refused to address me directly except to deliver a dressing down, which he did in the presence of others and with savage enjoyment. Whenever I brought him a letter for signature, he would recoil: not histrionically, but with the small fastidious shudder of one who fears contamination.

At first I was angry, vowing revenge on him, then hurt, then sad, for I missed him. As years passed, the hostility decayed to the point where we simply ignored each other's existence; then, to my relief and his own surprise, he was promoted. He became Keeper of Records and was moved two floors down to sit, solitary, in a room of his own, with only deeds and dead files to tyrannize. His enemies had won the sweetest of all victories. In times past, he had sneered when they rewarded flatterers and favourites with advancement; now, by virtuously giving him no less than his due they had exiled him to a miniature Siberia where he could lash out at the four walls, abuse the strongroom and wage a vendetta with the dust. They were rid of him.

I was clearing out my table to leave the Land Commission for good when someone said: 'You ought to go down to Records and say goodbye to Drumm.'

'Like hell I will.'

'Ah, do. Sure he's not the worst of them.'

'No, thank you. I'm not giving him another chance to insult me.'

'Ah, what odds? Say goodbye to him. Poor old bugger, but.'

In the end I went downstairs, if only because I knew that he no longer had the power to hurt me. Besides, today was the day I had dreamed of, and I was both maudlin with excitement and afflicted – then, as I still am – with an inability to leave a loose end or a piece of unfinished business. I knocked at his door, entered and saw him stiffen like an animal that sees a natural enemy. His Adam's apple dipped and rose in a contemptuous curtsey.

'What do you want?'

I said: 'I'm leaving now, Mr Drumm, and I thought I'd say goodbye.'

'Leaving?' His nostrils, those antennae of his, had begun to flare. 'What has that to do with me? And where, may I ask, are you going?'

I said: 'I've resigned. I'm leaving to write professionally.'

He looked down at his table and was silent. It was a mannerism I had seen a hundred times when he was pondering the next step in his strategy against a defaulting farmer. Then he said: 'Nobody tells me anything in this place,' and when he raised his head I saw with horror that a tear had begun to run down one cheek.

He shook my hand, blew his nose, wished me well, debated my prospects and said that I was doing the right thing. 'There's no future for you here. I told you that fourteen years ago.' Our quarrel was not mentioned.

I was to see him once more, six years later. I had come home from London for my mother's funeral and caught sight of him standing outside the church, his head bared, as the hearse and cars moved off. That afternoon, I escaped from the oppressiveness of the house and my father's bewilderment and took my daughter, then aged nine, for a walk. I knew that Mr Drumm had by now retired, and we called to his house on Dalkey Avenue. He was delighted to see us and turned at once to address the stairs: 'My dear, John has paid us a visit.' It was the first time he had called me by my given name. Mrs Drumm, when she hurried down, gave every evidence of amazement, not so much at the appearance of uninvited guests than at seeing her husband in a good humour. I heard later that she had provoked his displeasure in some way a few years previously and that now he spoke to her only when they had company. True or made up, I could believe it.

She brought tea and biscuits. Mr Drumm talked about my mother's illness, assured me sternly that I had no cause for self-reproach and made light of my misgivings as regards how my father would cope on his own. 'The old man,' Mr Drumm said, refusing to the end to grant him the status of a parent, 'will come to no great harm.' He complimented me on my progress as a playwright, and I promised to send him tickets for a play of mine that was due to be revived in Dublin. We took our leave, and a few weeks later I received a letter in the familiar writing, as spiky and upright as himself and signed 'John T. Drumm'. It was not merely a note of thanks but a formal and detailed critique of the play, written as if he were a professor to whom I, a student, had submitted a paper for marking. Oh, an impossible man.

My mother died an Irishwoman's death, drinking tea, a day or so after she had been admitted to hospital. She had had a heart attack in January and half sat, half lay in the small room downstairs that was used only at Christmas and on special occasions. One day in May, Mrs Pim called to see my father and give him his quarterly cheque. He was incoherent from two nights without sleep. She went into the front room, looked at my mother and returned saying: 'Keyes, do you realize she's dying?', then went out and telephoned for an ambulance.

He lived for another two years, stubbornly insisting that he could forage for himself and only dimly aware that he was being watched over from a discreet distance by the neighbours and his niece who lived near by. 'I blacked the range yesterday,' he would boast when I came to see him. 'And go out and look at the garden. Fine heads of cabbage that a dog from Dublin never pissed on.' He would hear no talk of his coming to live with us in London. 'What would I do the like of that for? And leave herself's bits and pieces here for any dog or divil to make off with?' Then he would go blathering about how he met Father Kearney in the town yesterday, who said to him that he was a marvel, so he was, and they'd have to shoot him in the wind-up. 'Aren't you great!' I would jeer, and 'I am!' he would answer proudly.

He began to show signs of senility. He called to my cousin Rosie's for his Christmas dinner at two in the morning. Past and present became one to him. He would sing out the names of the roses he had grown for the Jacobs: Cornelias and Belles de Crecys, Tuscanys and Amy Robsarts, New Dawns and King's Ransoms. He was a young fellow again, asking to marry my mother, telling her father that he had a pound a week and the promise of one of the new cottages in the Square. He would stand in Castle Street in full day, stormy and ranting as if he had held back an inner rage all his life and now it was spilling out. A friend telephoned me.

'There's certain people been complaining about him,' he said. 'Saying he's a public nuisance and ought to be put in care.'

'What certain people?' I said. 'Do I know them?'

'You might,' he said. 'An old bollix called Drumm.'

Drumm. At his name the furnace of my old hatred for him blazed up again. I silently screamed for him to get out of my life, and my rage was all the greater for knowing that he was in the right. I asked a doctor friend if I should bring my father to London, like it or not. He said: 'And then what? He'll get worse and be sent to hospital and die there, in Wandsworth or Putney, with nothing around him that's Irish except perhaps the nurses.' So my cousins arranged for him to live in a house that was part hotel, part old people's home. It was half a mile from the town, and we comforted ourselves that on his good days he could walk to Mass, to the bookie's or to buy his tobacco. The time was past for good days, however, and one night he somehow managed to climb the front wall in his determination to get to the bank with one of the cheques I sent him. When two nurses tried to bring him back he assaulted them, and I was duly informed that the management declined to continue to harbour an eighty-three-year-old delinquent. His next and last stop was a psychiatric hospital where he died, a sister told me, 'like a bird'. Mr Drumm died the same year, almost as if contented that he had outlived his rival.

Two years later, in 1970, we returned to Ireland for good. My wife and daughter travelled back by air, while I drove the car to Liverpool and caught the ferry. Rain poured down in sheets as the lights along the Mersey grew smaller and blinked out, but in Dublin the morning sunlight was a knife against the eyes. A customs officer looked at the documents that told him I was importing my car for purposes of residence. He said: 'You're welcome back', and I drove out of the shed and towards the city centre. A few people were about, their eyes sleep-filled. Away to the south were the three hills, Dalkey, Killiney and Mullins's, as blue-grey and fine as bits of Wedgewood, and I remembered another journey home, long ago.

I was seven or eight and had gone, one October afternoon, with some other boys to an estate called Belton's to gather sticks for firewood. Trees had been felled the day before, and we ranged like scavengers along the field's edge, grubbing for the thickest branches and breaking them with boot and knee. I would look around from time to time and see the others, like distant crows pecking at cow pats, but when I had at last loaded the box cart that my father had made for me from two butter boxes and a pair of pram wheels, I realized that they had all gone and it was getting dark. I had never been out so late on my own and so far from home. I pushed the box cart across the ruts of the field, through the haze and autumn smell of a bonfire and then along Ballinclea Road where, so they said, there was a ghost in the shape of a black dog. It was not the dog I was afraid of, but the failing light. I knew that at all costs I must get home before night, and I began to run, racing the dark.

The wheels jumped and skittered; twigs from my load fell off into the road. It was that last moment of day when the wind drops and nothing moves, the instant of stillness before a shout. Lights were coming on in the houses: I saw a man, a coloured picture in a black frame, reading his newspaper by the fire and, further along, a table laid for tea. I ran harder. In our own house I saw my father, home from work, pick up the alarm clock that lay on its back on the dresser and turn it this way and that, as if it would tell him what had become of me; I heard the gas purr in the mantle and saw the tea in the cups, and the bread, buttered and waiting; I saw my mother at the corner of the lane, peering down Sorrento Road for a sight of me, one hand comforting the other. I wanted to tell them: I'm not far, I'm hurrying. I ran down Spring Hill, along Barnhill Road, past the Metals, through the town and towards the last turn of the road, towards the two lighted rooms that were the harbour at the world's end.

FOR THE BEST IN PAPERBACKS, LOOK FOR THE

In every corner of the world, on every subject under the sun, Penguin represents quality and variety – the very best in publishing today.

For complete information about books available from Penguin – including Pelicans, Puffins, Peregrines and Penguin Classics – and how to order them, write to us at the appropriate address below. Please note that for copyright reasons the selection of books varies from country to country.

In the United Kingdom: Please write to *Dept E.P., Penguin Books Ltd, Harmondsworth, Middlesex, UB7 0DA*

In the United States: Please write to *Dept BA, Penguin, 299 Murray Hill Parkway, East Rutherford, New Jersey 07073*

In Canada: Please write to *Penguin Books Canada Ltd, 2801 John Street, Markham, Ontario L3R 1B4*

In Australia: Please write to the *Marketing Department, Penguin Books Australia Ltd, P.O. Box 257, Ringwood, Victoria 3134*

In New Zealand: Please write to the *Marketing Department, Penguin Books (NZ) Ltd, Private Bag, Takapuna, Auckland 9*

In India: Please write to *Penguin Overseas Ltd, 706 Eros Apartments, 56 Nehru Place, New Delhi, 110019*

In Holland: Please write to *Penguin Books Nederland B.V., Postbus 195, NL–1380AD Weesp, Netherlands*

In Germany: Please write to *Penguin Books Ltd, Friedrichstrasse 10–12, D–6000 Frankfurt Main 1, Federal Republic of Germany*

In Spain: Please write to *Longman Penguin España, Calle San Nicolas 15, E–28013 Madrid, Spain*

In France: Please write to *Penguin Books Ltd, 39 Rue de Montmorency, F-75003, Paris, France*

In Japan: Please write to *Longman Penguin Japan Co Ltd, Yamaguchi Building, 2–12–9 Kanda Jimbocho, Chiyoda-Ku, Tokyo 101, Japan*

A CHOICE OF PENGUINS

The Diary of Virginia Woolf
Five volumes edited by Quentin Bell and Anne Olivier Bell

'As an account of intellectual and cultural life of our century, Virginia Woolf's diaries are invaluable; as the record of one bruised and unquiet mind, they are unique' – Peter Ackroyd in the *Sunday Times*

Voices of the Old Sea   Norman Lewis

'I will wager that *Voices of the Old Sea* will be a classic in the literature about Spain' – *Mail on Sunday* 'Limpidly and lovingly Norman Lewis has caught the helpless, unwitting, often foolish, but always hopeful village in its dying summers, and saved the tragedy with sublime comedy' – *Observer*

The First World War   A J P Taylor

In this superb illustrated history, A J P Taylor 'manages to say almost everything that is important for an understanding and, indeed, intellectual digestion of that vast event . . . A special text . . . a remarkable collection of photographs' – *Observer*

Ninety-Two Days   Evelyn Waugh

With characteristic honesty Evelyn Waugh here debunks the romantic notions attached to rough travelling; his journey in Guiana and Brazil is difficult, dangerous and extremely uncomfortable, and his account of it is witty and unquestionably compelling.

When the Mind Hears   Harlan Lane
A History of the Deaf

'Reads like a suspense novel . . . what emerges is evidence of a great wrong done to a minority group, the deaf' – *The New York Times Book Review* 'Impassioned, polemical, at times even virulent . . . (he shows) immense scholarship, powers of historical reconstruction, and deep empathy for the world of the deaf' – Oliver Sacks in *The New York Review of Books*

A CHOICE OF PENGUINS

Fantastic Invasion   Patrick Marnham

Explored and exploited, Africa has carried a different meaning for each wave of foreign invaders – from ivory traders to aid workers. Now, in the crisis that has followed Independence, which way should Africa turn? 'A courageous and brilliant effort' – Paul Theroux

Jean Rhys: Letters 1931–66
Edited by Francis Wyndham and Diana Melly

'Eloquent and invaluable . . . her life emerges, and with it a portrait of an unexpectedly indomitable figure' – Marina Warner in the *Sunday Times*

Among the Russians   Colin Thubron

One man's solitary journey by car across Russia provides an enthralling and revealing account of the habits and idiosyncrasies of a fascinating people. 'He sees things with the freshness of an innocent and the erudition of a scholar' – *Daily Telegraph*

The Amateur Naturalist   Gerald Durrell with Lee Durrell

'Delight . . . on every page . . . packed with authoritative writing, learning without pomposity . . . it represents a real bargain' – *The Times Educational Supplement*. 'What treats are in store for the average British household' – *Books and Bookmen*

The Democratic Economy   Geoff Hodgson

Today, the political arena is divided as seldom before. In this exciting and original study, Geoff Hodgson carefully examines the claims of the rival doctrines and exposes some crucial flaws.

They Went to Portugal   Rose Macaulay

An exotic and entertaining account of travellers to Portugal from the pirate-crusaders, through poets, aesthetes and ambassadors, to the new wave of romantic travellers. A wonderful mixture of literature, history and adventure, by one of our most stylish and seductive writers.

BIOGRAPHY AND AUTOBIOGRAPHY IN PENGUIN

Jackdaw Cake Norman Lewis

From Carmarthen to Cuba, from Enfield to Algeria, Norman Lewis brilliantly recounts his transformation from stammering schoolboy to the man Auberon Waugh called 'the greatest travel writer alive, if not the greatest since Marco Polo'.

Catherine Maureen Dunbar

Catherine is the tragic story of a young woman who died of anorexia nervosa. Told by her mother, it includes extracts from Catherine's diary and conveys both the physical and psychological traumas suffered by anorexics.

Isak Dinesen, the Life of Karen Blixen Judith Thurman

Myth-spinner and storyteller famous far beyond her native Denmark, Karen Blixen lived much of the Gothic strangeness of her tales. This remarkable biography paints Karen Blixen in all her sybiline beauty and magnetism, conveying the delight and terror she inspired, and the pain she suffered.

The Silent Twins Marjorie Wallace

June and Jennifer Gibbons are twenty-three year old identical twins, who from childhood have been locked together in a strange secret bondage which made them reject the outside world. *The Silent Twins* is a real-life psychological thriller about the most fundamental question – what makes a separate, individual human being?

Backcloth Dirk Bogarde

The final volume of Dirk Bogarde's autobiography is not about his acting years but about Dirk Bogarde the man and the people and events that have shaped his life and character. All are remembered with affection, nostalgia and characteristic perception and eloquence.